JOHN PAUL II:

THE GREAT MERCY

POPE

John Paul II:

The Great Mercy Pope

Rev. George W. Kosicki, C.S.B.

John Paul II Institute of Divine Mercy
An imprint of *Marian Press*
Marians of the Immaculate Conception
Stockbridge, Massachusetts 01262

2004

NIHIL OBSTAT:
Rev. Richard J. Drabik, M.I.C.
June 25, 2001

IMPRIMI POTEST:
Very Rev. Walter F. Dziordz, M.I.C.
June 28, 2001
(Feast of Sts. Peter and Paul)

Library of Congress Catalog Number
2001093026

ISBN 0-944203-60-4

Editor: Robert Stackpole, STD
Proofreader: Carol Dickens
Typesetting: Patricia Menatti
Cover Design: William Sosa
Special Thanks: To Mr. Shaun Hillary,
for his generous help and prayers

Published by
John Paul II Institute of Divine Mercy
An Imprint of Marian Press

Table of Contents

Appendix

In Chronological Order:

Mercy Gems from John Paul II

- "Right from the beginning of my ministry in St. Peter's See in Rome, I considered this message [of Divine Mercy] my special task. Providence has assigned it to me in the present situation of man, the Church and the world. It could be said that precisely this situation assigned that message to me as my task before God" (November 22, 1981, Shrine of Merciful Love in Collevalenza, Italy).

- "On the threshold of the third millennium, I come to entrust to Him once more my Petrine ministry – 'Jesus, I trust in You!' ... I took with me [the message of Divine Mercy] to the See of Peter and which in a sense forms the image of this Pontificate" (Shrine of Divine Mercy, Krakow-Lagiewniki, Poland, June 7, 1997).

- "John Paul II, who said that he felt spiritually 'very near' to Sr. Faustina, had been 'thinking about her for a long time' when he began writing *Dives in Misericordia*" (George Weigel, *Witness to Hope*, 1999).

- "I will sing of the mercies of the Lord forever" (Psalm 89:2, John Paul II repeated on highlights of his papacy and at the canonization of St. Faustina, April 30, 2000).

- "Sr. Faustina's canonization has a particular eloquence: by this act, I intend today to pass this message on to the third millennium (Homily of Canonization of St. Faustina, April 30, 2000).

- "This is the happiest day of my life" (the Pope's words to Dr. Valentin Fuster – the cardiologist who investigated the miraculous healing of the heart of Fr. Ron Pytel through the intercession of St. Faustina – on the day of her canonization, April 30, 2000).

Preface

I have benefited from the priestly ministry and wisdom of Father George W. Kosicki, C.S.B. since I was a young priest, some thirty years ago. It was he who first introduced me to the valuable distinction between our soul and our spirit, which has proven to be of great service to me in many ways. From the mid-seventies to the early eighties, I derived great profit from my sojourns at Bethany House of Intercession where Father George and the other members of the core group welcomed all priests as their brothers and provided an atmosphere for prayer that was genuinely Catholic, wholesome and open to the impulses of the Spirit. For me – and I'm sure I can also speak for many others – Bethany furnished a real model of how to grow in priestly holiness by interceding for, serving and loving our brother priests.

It was during an extended period at Bethany, at the very beginning of the pontificate of Pope John Paul II, that I was spurred on by Father George and his brethren to consecrate myself to Our Lady, an act of incalculable importance in my life as a Christian and as a priest. It was during that same period at Bethany that Father George and Father Seraphim Michalenko, M.I.C. introduced me to the life and writings of Sister Maria Faustina Kowalska whose beatification on April 18, 1993 and canonization on April 30, 2000 I had the joy of attending. Their writings on Saint Faustina have proven to be a great enrichment in my own spiritual life.

I must also credit Father George with helping me to appreciate the Polish background of Pope John Paul II and to savor the richness and originality of so much of his prophetic teaching and example. In a certain sense, then, I am also indebted to Father George for helping to launch me on my own studies of the teachings of this extraordinary pontiff on Marian consecration as in so many other areas. Hence, I am pleased to have this opportunity to offer a word of commendation on Father

George's work on John Paul II, whom he aptly describes as "the Mercy Pope".

It is well known that the Church never defines a doctrine or approves a devotion on the basis of a private revelation. In his monumental Encyclical Letter *Haurietis Aquas* on devotion to the Most Sacred Heart of Jesus, Pope Pius XII was at pains to point out that the devotion to the Heart of Jesus is solidly grounded in the Scriptures and the Church's millennial tradition and has not "taken its origin from some private revelation", even if it cannot be denied that the revelations to Saint Margaret Mary in the seventeenth century provided the most powerful impetus for its promotion. As John Paul II himself put it in his letter to Father Hans-Peter Kolvenbach, the Superior General of the Jesuits, of 5 October 1986:

> In fact, if the Lord in his providence wished that a powerful drive in favour of the devotion to the Heart of Christ, under the forms indicated in the revelations received by St. Margaret Mary, should go forth from Paray-le-Monial in the seventeenth century, at the threshold of modern times, *the essential elements of this devotion belong in a permanent fashion to the spirituality of the Church throughout her history* (emphasis mine).

The same holds true for the devotion to The Divine Mercy. Even if the greatest stimulus for the devotion comes from the *Diary* of Saint Faustina, it must be recognized that the bases are deeply rooted in Scripture and Tradition and clearly indicated in theology and the magisterium. The writings of Saint Faustina are a confirmation of the public revelation which has been entrusted to the Church, not its source. Hence John Paul II's Encyclical Letter *Dives in Misericordia* of November 30, 1980 is rightly based on the sources of public revelation and not on the private revelations to Sister Faustina with which the Pope was already surely very familiar. The Pope wisely presented the Church's doctrine on Divine Mercy and its vocation to be a messenger of mercy and intercessor for it with no explicit references to the writings of Saint Faustina. This provided a necessary dogmatic exposition of the mystery of God's unfathomable mercy which would effectively verify the insights which the Lord gave to the Polish nun whose cause for canonization he had presented as Archbishop of Krakow and whom he raised to the honors of the altar as Pope.

Father Kosicki's present work is a notable contribution to the literature on this theme precisely because in it he makes available in one convenient volume the rich patrimony of the Holy Father's teaching on Divine Mercy as he has consistently taught and preached about it in the exercise of his ordinary magisterium (cf. the Second Vatican Council's Dogmatic Constitution on the Church, *Lumen Gentium #25*) from the time of his election as Successor of Peter up until Divine Mercy Sunday 2001. Thus, this book is a veritable treasure trove for theologians as well as for all of the faithful. But it is not just a compilation. It is also a book rich in insights which are the fruit of Father George's extended prayer and study and presented with his conspicuous gifts as a master teacher. It is a book which makes me grateful anew for Pope John Paul II's Petrine teaching ministry as well as for the priestly ministry of Father George W. Kosicki.

Rev. Msgr. Arthur B. Calkins

Foreword

In his book, John Paul II: the Great Mercy Pope, Father George Kosicki explores the message of God's mercy in the writings and speeches of our Holy Father, Pope John Paul II. While this book is about the present day Peter and his message to the world, it is really about the journey of a man of faith, prayer and illumination, which comes from contemplation, who, in his own life and the life of his native land of Poland, came to believe in and proclaim the mercy of God to the whole world. He has proclaimed God's mercy in word and deed. Because of his universal appeal and because of the message of his pontificate, the message of God's mercy which is God's greatest attribute, John Paul II may one day be known as John Paul the Great.

While the pontificate of John Paul II gives him the world stage as his arena to proclaim the message of mercy, it is a message that reaches back to his youth. As a young college student in Krakow, he witnessed man's inhumanity to man during World War II in occupied Poland. He saw many people rounded up and sent to concentration camps and slave labor. In his home town of Wadowice, he had many friends of the Jewish faith who would perish in the holocaust. Death and danger surrounded the young Wojtyla. He experienced the need for God's mercy and humanity's need to be merciful to one another.

It was during this horrible period in human history that the young Karol Wojtyla decided to enter Cardinal Sapieha's clandestine seminary in Krakow. This decision further jeopardized his life, for he could be executed if caught. It was also during this time that another seminarian, Andrew Deskur, now a retired Cardinal at the Vatican, introduced Karol to the message of the Divine Mercy, as revealed to the mystic nun, now Saint Maria Faustina. Sister Faustina's convent was in the suburbs of Krakow in an area called Łagiewniki. This mystic nun, a suffering soul, who died at the age of 33 in 1938, wrote a diary entitled "Divine Mercy in My Soul", in which she recorded the revelations given to her by Jesus about the greatness of God's mercy. The message of God's mercy, as recorded by Sister Faustina, would be a beacon of light and hope for the people of Poland during this dark time in their history.

In his future years as a young priest and later as Bishop and Archbishop of Krakow, now under the oppression of a communist regime, Karol Wojtyla would reflect and meditate upon the message of God's mercy. He would often visit the convent in Lagiewniki where Sister Faustina was buried for private times of prayer and to lead the Sisters in reflective retreats.

Due to an erroneous translation of Sister Faustina's diary, a Vatican ban was imposed upon "the spread of images and writings that propose the devotion of the Divine Mercy in the form proposed by the same Sister Faustina." In 1965 however, because of popular desire, Archbishop Wojtyla conferred with Cardinal Ottaviani to have Sister Faustina raised to the honor of the altar. Cardinal Ottaviani urged the Archbishop to begin an investigation while there were still living witnesses to the sanctity of Sister Faustina. Archbishop Wojtyla immediately delegated Bishop Julian Groblicki to begin the informative process into the heroic virtues of Sister Maria Faustina Kowalska. On September 20, 1967, the Archbishop of Krakow, now Karol Cardinal Wojtyla, officially closed the first informative stage in the process for the beatification of the Servant of God, Sister Faustina Kowalska. The results of the informative process showed that earlier action taken by Rome regarding the message of Divine Mercy as proposed by Sister Faustina was taken on insufficient evidence. On January 31, 1968, the process of beatification of Sister Faustina was formally inaugurated. On April 15, 1978, the prohibitions by the Vatican were lifted. Six months later, on October 16, 1978, Karol Cardinal Wojtyla was elected as Pope John Paul II.

Pope John Paul II felt that the keynote of his pontificate was to spread the message of God's infinite mercy. Father Kosicki very ably explores that message in both the writings and talks of our Holy Father. It is a message of hope for the new millennium. John Paul II not only proclaims this message, he lives it, and he calls the Church to live it. He lived the virtue of mercy when he forgave his would-be assassin, Ali Agca, in his prison cell on December 27, 1983; he continues to live the virtue of mercy in his care for the poor, the ill, and the down-trodden; and now he lives the virtue of mercy in his own personal suffering, which he offers for the salvation of souls.

On December 21, 1992, John Paul II had the privilege of publishing the Church's acceptance of the miracle through the intercession of Sister Faustina which paved the way for her beatification on April 18, 1993, the first Sunday after Easter, the Sunday on which, as had been revealed to Sister Faustina by our Lord, the Feast of His Mercy (Mercy Sunday) was to be celebrated.

On October 5, 1995, the feast day of Blessed Faustina, I experienced a total healing of my severely damaged heart after praying for her intercession. During the investigative process regarding my healing, I had the privilege of meeting Pope John Paul II on two different occasions. I can personally say that he is a man of deep prayer who emanates sanctity and deep compassion. On December 20, 1999, Pope John Paul II accepted my healing as the miracle for the canonization of Blessed Faustina. On April 30, 2000, Pope John Paul II canonized St. Maria Faustina Kowalska as the first saint of the new millennium. He also proclaimed Mercy Sunday as a universal feast for the Church. He held up St. Faustina and her message of and devotion to The Divine Mercy as a model for the Church. At a dinner following the canonization ceremony, Pope John Paul II told Dr. Valentine Fuster, a pre-eminent cardiologist who studied my case for months and who served on the team of medical consultants for the Congregation for the Causes of Saints, "this is the happiest day of my life".

It was through a simple Polish nun, called to be the Apostle and Secretary of The Divine Mercy, that the world has been called to pray for mercy, be merciful and have complete trust in the Lord. It was a message first for Poland, and then for the whole world.

It is because of many years of prayer and contemplation on God's great mercy, that the first Polish Pope has been able to proclaim the same message in word and deed. As a former drama student and now as Pope, Karol Wojtyla became, in many ways, the greatest actor on the world stage at the end of the twentieth century. His greatest contribution to humanity, however, is the fulfillment of our Lord's wishes to St. Faustina, namely, that the message of the Divine Mercy be spread around the world. St. Faustina began this mission. Pope John Paul II has continued it. He led the Church into the new millennium, which he sees as a new Pentecost, with two messages of wisdom: "Fear not!" and "Trust in the Lord". That is why John Paul II may one day be known as John Paul the Great: the Mercy Pope.

Give thanks to the Lord, for He is good.

Give thanks to the Lord for He is merciful.

Rev. Ronald P. Pytel

Introduction

Pope John Paul II has accomplished so much during his pontificate that he may one day be given the title "John Paul the Great" by the Universal Church. He has been seen by vast numbers of people around the world, gathering the largest single assembly of people in human history, – over 5 million in the Philippines – gathering millions of the young and electrifying them. He has written and taught by numerous encyclicals and apostolic documents on Jesus Christ, the truth of the Gospel, the creed, natural law, human reason, sacredness of life, and social justice. He has published best selling books; initiated the Catechism of the Catholic Church; he inspired the non-violent liberation of Eastern Europe from communist oppression; he has guided the Church through the celebration of the Jubilee Year 2000.

One of the outstanding achievements of John Paul II, according to his biographer George Weigel, the author of *Witness to Hope*, is the pope's use of the "Law of the Gift" – the total self-gift of love of the Father and Son in the Spirit that gives life. Out of this total love, God created man in His own image, male and female (see Genesis 1:27), in order that we may receive His love and give love to one another and so give new life in the image of God. God's plan is to have families that share in his very love and life. This teaching of John Paul II on human sexuality and marriage could revolutionize family life in the modern world, returning it to its roots in the divine plan.

When man rebelled and spoiled God's plan, God promised an alternate plan. Out of His infinite, merciful love, God sent His only Son to offer His life and love for the forgiveness of our sins, for our redemption and for our eternal life. This mercy is God's love poured out upon us and is a special expression of the "Law of the Gift". This is the great mercy that John Paul II has conveyed in his writings and proclaimed in his preaching.

In this book, *John Paul II: the Great Mercy Pope*, we will see how the Holy Father has not only taught about God's mercy, but also how he has lived out the message of mercy by the witness of his life. In his writing, teaching, preaching, and by his prayer, his forgiveness, his radiating presence and his ministry to the sick and poor, he reflects God's mercy. The very themes of his pontificate are mercy themes: his challenge, "Do not be afraid!" his call to holiness, to evangelization, to ecumenism; his entrustment to The Divine Mercy and to the Mother of Mercy; the Jubilee Year of mercy; his continued emphasis on the value and dignity of every human being. For all these things, John Paul II has shown himself to be the Mercy Pope. His whole life, therefore, should be an example for the world and a challenge to each individual to be merciful as our heavenly Father is merciful.

Part I: Teacher of Mercy

Chapter 1: The Encyclical Rich in Mercy
(*Dives in Misericordia*)

The opening line of John Paul II's second encyclical sets the tone and summarizes the document:

> It is God, who is rich in mercy (Eph. 2:4) whom Jesus Christ has revealed to us as Father.

The encyclical concludes that the mission of Christ is also the mission of His Church:

> The reason for her existence is, in fact, to reveal God, that Father who allows Himself to be "seen" in Christ (cf Jn.14:9).

This encyclical is a teaching and proclamation on the nature of Divine Mercy that builds up to an exhortation to pray for mercy for the whole world and concludes with John Paul II leading us in a strong prayer for mercy. This special prayer of the Pope will be discussed in Chapter Four.

The origins of the knowledge and concern of Pope John Paul II for the message of Divine Mercy come from his personal involvement with the message of Divine Mercy revealed to Sister Faustina Kowalska (1905-1938) in his home archdiocese of Krakow, Poland. During the 1930's, Sister Faustina received revelations from our Lord telling her of His infinite mercy for mankind. He asked that His mercy be made known to everyone now, "while it still is the time for mercy." As Archbishop of Krakow, the then Karol Wojtyla introduced Sister Faustina's cause for canonization. He was instrumental in conscripting the leading Polish theologian, the Reverend Professor Ignacy Róż ycki, to prepare a definitive study of her writings and of the heroic virtues of her life. After ten years of exhaustive study, Professor Różycki submitted a highly favorable document of support for the cause of her canonization.

George Weigel in his *Witness to Hope*, the biography of Pope John Paul II, recorded a remarkable statement of the Holy Father, associating Sr. Faustina and his encyclical on Divine Mercy :

> As Archbishop of Krakow, Wojtyla had defended Sister Faustina when her orthodoxy was being posthumously questioned in Rome, due in large part to a faulty Italian translation of her diary, and had promoted the cause of her beatification. John Paul II, who said that he felt spiritually "very near" to Sister Faustina, had been "thinking about her for a long time" when he began *Dives in Misericordia.*

A Trilogy of Encyclicals:

Three encyclicals of Pope John Paul II form a trilogy, as he himself expressed in the third letter. The first letter, *Redeemer of Man* points to Jesus Christ as "the center of history and the universe" who reveals to each and every person their identity and dignity. He further points out that the Church is the link and the way to Christ for every person in every circumstance of life. The second letter of the trilogy is *Rich in Mercy*, in which John Paul II points to the Father as rich in mercy. The Father's mercy is revealed in Christ Jesus, Mercy Incarnate, the only hope for peace in the world. In the third letter of the trilogy, *Lord and Giver of Life*, John Paul II shows that it is the Holy Spirit who converts us from our greatest sin, namely, the practical atheism of the world. At the same time, he shows that the Holy Spirit brings our souls to the cross to be washed in the blood of Jesus, so that we might receive His saving love and mercy and inherit eternal life.

This trilogy is a clear response to the greatest problems of our day. Sin is the issue of our day, and mercy is the answer.

Summaries of the encyclical on Divine Mercy

Because of its importance, three kinds of summaries of the

encyclical are presented here as aids to understanding the message:

An "Abstract" which gives the sequence of the topics and the flow of the main concepts;

A "Schematic Summary" which gathers the key points in sweeping statements that can be used to teach, preach, and be reminders of this message of mercy; and

A "Sense-line Summary" which stresses the main points of each section in short phrases, conveying the strength of the message.

Abstract

The theme of the encyclical letter *Dives in Misericordia* is Divine Mercy. Pope John Paul II develops the thesis that *to practice, proclaim, and pray for mercy is the mission of the Church and the whole world.* The letter is divided into eight chapters with fifteen sub-topics.

In Chapter One, the Pope expands the biblical text Jn. 14:9, "He who sees me sees the Father," by discussing the revelation of mercy through Christ, the incarnation of mercy. He encourages us all to open our minds and hearts more widely to Christ.

"The Messianic Message" of Chapter Two describes "When Christ Began To Do and To Teach." The Messiah is a clear sign of God who is love. Through His lifestyle and through His actions, Jesus revealed that love is present in the world.

"The Old Testament" is the topic of Chapter Three. The concept of mercy and its history are developed. Mercy is contrasted with God's justice.

"The Parable of the Prodigal Son" is the topic of Chapter Four. It brings focus to the relationship between justice and love that is manifested as mercy. In this parable, love is transformed into mercy. A particular focus on human dignity is presented, as well as the faithfulness of a Father's love.

In "The Paschal Mystery," Chapter Five, mercy is revealed in the Cross and Resurrection. It emphasizes that love is present in the world and that this love is more powerful than any kind of evil. Believing in this love means believing in mercy. "Love More Powerful Than Death, More Powerful Than Sin" is expanded. A discussion of Mary, the Blessed Mother of Jesus and the "Mother of Mercy" concludes the chapter.

Chapter Six proclaims "Mercy ... from Generation to Generation" and discusses the need for mercy in our generation. There are sources of uneasiness and a lack of peace attributed to our times. The question, "Is Justice Enough?" is raised. The Pope calls for a deeper power of love, for justice is *not* enough.

"The Mercy of God in the Mission of the Church" stresses the Church's role to profess and proclaim the mercy of God, the most stupendous attribute of the Creator and Redeemer. "The Church Seeks to Put Mercy into Practice" for "blessed are the merciful, for they shall obtain mercy." True mercy is, so to speak, the most profound source of justice. Mercy is also the most perfect incarnation of "equality" between people. All people are invited to proclaim and introduce into life the mystery of mercy supremely revealed in Jesus Christ. "It is precisely in the name of this mystery that Christ teaches us to forgive always. ...he who forgives and he who is forgiven encounter one another at an essential point, namely, the dignity or essential value of the person...".

The encyclical letter ends with "The Prayer of the Church in Our Times." Prayer is needed to overcome modern man's lack of courage to utter the word "mercy." The Pope exhorts us to call upon the God who loves all people and desires every true good for each individual. He prays that the Love which is in the Father may once again be revealed at this stage of history. He concludes by pointing out that the very reason for the Church's existence is to reveal God, who is Love and Mercy Itself.

Schematic Summary of "Rich in Mercy"

The Papal Letter "Rich in Mercy" proclaims mercy as:

THE revelation of the Father, who is rich in mercy.

THE prophetic word for our times.

THE power and mission of Christ and His Church.

THE summary of the Gospel: "Blessed are the merciful, for they shall obtain mercy."

THE parable of mercy: the Prodigal Son – the essence of mercy in the restored value of man.

THE answer to the anxiety of "a lack of peace."

THE summons to the Church and by the Church to practice, preach, and plead for mercy.

THE revelation of Jesus, Mercy Incarnate, centered in the crucified and risen Jesus, and continued in the Heart of Mary.

THE prayer for the presence of love, which is greater than evil, sin and death.

THE plea for us and the whole world.

A Sense-Line Summary of "Rich in Mercy"

I.   He who sees me sees the Father

Jesus
has revealed God
who is rich in mercy
as the Father.

Christ crucified
is the center of all;
He reveals to us
the mercy
of the Father. (1)

God is visible
in and through Christ,
visible in His mercy.
Christ is mercy,
incarnate and personified.
Is mercy a threat?
No.
God is the Father of mercies
especially to the suffering.
This letter is a summons
TO the Church and
BY the Church
for mercy. (2)

II.   The Messianic Message

When Christ began
to do and teach,
He proclaimed
liberty to the oppressed.
The words and actions of Jesus
make the Father present,
the Father who is love and mercy.
Jesus demanded from the people
the same love and mercy
as a condition of mercy:
"The merciful....shall obtain mercy." (3)

III.   The Old Testament

The Hebrew Bible
is a history of special experiences
of the mercy of the Lord.
Mercy is a special power of love
which prevails over the sin
and infidelity of the chosen people.
Mercy is the content of the

experience of intimacy
with their Lord.
Mercy is *Hesed*:
goodness, grace, love, fidelity.

Mercy is *Rahamim:*
love of a mother, tender, the heart's womb.
The Old Testament
encourages the suffering to appeal
to mercy.
Mercy is more powerful
and more profound than justice.
Mercy is love vis-a-vis justice.
Mercy is involved in the mystery of creation
and in the mystery of election. (4)

IV   The Parable of the Prodigal Son

Mary's canticle brings Old Testament mercy
to the New Testament:
"mercy... from generation to generation."
Zachariah's canticle remembers
God's covenant of mercy,
both "hesed" and "rahamim."
The parable of the Prodigal Son
expresses the essence of Divine Mercy.
Each of us
in each age
is the prodigal.
The dignity of the son
in the father's house
is greater than his possessions
or their lack.
The son's turning point
is the awareness
of the loss of his dignity
as his father's son.

Love is transformed into mercy
as it goes beyond
the precise norm of justice. (5).

The father is faithful
to his fatherhood.
The son's humanity is saved.
Mercy has the interior form
of agape-love.
The son is restored
to value
and not humiliated.

Conversion
is the most concrete working of mercy
in the human world.
Mercy restores value,
promotes good,
draws good from evil,
causes rejoicing.
Mercy is the fundamental
content and power
of Christ's mission. (6)

V.   The Paschal Mystery

The Father in Christ's Paschal Mystery
reveals the depth of love
and the greatness of man.
The Paschal Mystery
is a superabundance
of justice
that bears upon sin and
restores love.
It reveals mercy in its fullness.
The Cross is the final word
of Christ's messianic mission,

speaking unceasingly of God
the Father as
merciful.
Believing in the crucified Son
is believing in love
present in the world.
Believing in the crucified Son
is believing in mercy.

The Cross is witness
to the strength of evil
in the world.
In Christ on the Cross
Justice is done
to sin and death
at the price
of sacrifice and death.
The Cross is
the radical revelation
of mercy.
The Resurrection perfects
the revelation of mercy and
foretells a new heaven.
In this our time,
love is revealed as mercy.
In the end,
mercy will be revealed as love.

The Church's program,
like Christ's mission
is mercy.
With the Cross at the center,
Christ crucified is the Word
that does not pass away.
He is the one who stands at the door
and knocks. (7).

Our love of God
is an act of mercy
toward the incarnate Son of the Father.
"Blessed are the merciful,
for they shall obtain mercy"
is a synthesis
of the whole Good News.
By the Resurrection
Jesus experienced mercy –
the very love of the Father –
more powerful than death!
In the Paschal Mystery
Christ reveals himself
as the inexhaustible source
of mercy –
He is the definitive incarnation
of mercy;
its living sign. (8)

In this age, too,
"His mercy is from generation to generation..."
Mary, who obtained mercy
like no other
shares in revealing
God's mercy
by the sacrifice of her heart.
Mary experienced
the mystery of Mercy
and also has the deepest knowledge
of mercy.
She knows its price.
She received into her heart
the mystery of mercy.
Mary is the Mother of Mercy.
What Jesus came to reveal,
her heart continues to reveal

as the merciful love
of a mother. (9)

VI.   Mercy ... from generation to generation

Our generation, too,
is included
in His mercy.
This age has tremendous potential
but
there is a lack of peace and
a sense of powerlessness
in regard to the situation
in the world. (10)

There is increasing fear
of destruction
because of atomic stockpiles;
fear of oppression
because of materialism
and abuse of power.
There is a gigantic remorse
over inequity
between rich and poor nations.
This is why
the moral lack of peace
is destined to become
even more acute.
This lack of peace
reaches out for solutions.
This lack of peace
is stronger
than all emergency measures. (11)

Justice alone
is not enough!
The Church shares with the people

the desire for a just life.
Often programs that start
with the idea of justice
suffer in practice
from distortions.
The Church shares
in the lack of peace
caused by the decline
of fundamental values,
the crisis in truth,
desacralization of relationships
and the common good. (12)

VII.   The Mercy of God in the Mission of the Church

In the face of the lack of peace,
the Church must witness
to mercy
by professing
and proclaiming it.

Mercy is
the greatest attribute of God
towards His people.
The Heart of Christ
is the center of the revelation
of the merciful love
of the Father.
The Church lives authentic life
when she draws near
to the source, Christ's Heart,
and dispenses
and professes mercy.
Mercy is
the most stupendous attribute
of the Creator and Redeemer.
The sources

of the Savior's mercy are:
the Word of God;
Eucharist – love more powerful than death
Reconciliation – love greater than sin.
God, who is love
cannot reveal Himself
other than as Mercy.
Mercy, like God,
is infinite –
infinite in readiness
and power to forgive.
Conversion –
consists in the discovery
of mercy and
a rediscovery of the Father. (13)

"Blessed are the merciful,
for they shall obtain mercy."
Man attains God's mercy
as he is merciful.
Mercy is
reciprocal and bilateral –
the one who gives
is also the beneficiary.
As man respects
the dignity of man,
Christ receives mercy
as done unto Himself.
Mercy is the most profound source of justice
and the most perfect incarnation
of the "equality" of justice.
Mercy makes
the world more human
because it introduces
forgiveness.
The Church must proclaim

and introduce mercy –
the source of forgiveness
from our wellspring, the Savior.
Forgiveness is for everyone –
for all time –
not a cancellation
of the requirement of justice,
not an indulgence
toward evil
but the love necessary so that
man may affirm himself
as man –
as the father affirmed
the dignity
of his prodigal son. (14)

VIII.   The Prayer of the Church in our Times

The church must proclaim
and practice mercy.
Yet,
in these critical times,
she cannot forget
the right and duty
to appeal for mercy–
especially when the world
moves away from mercy.
"Loud cries" for mercy
ought to be the cry
of the Church of our times.
Modern man is anxious
about the solution
to the terrible tensions
of our times, and lack of courage
to cry for mercy.
So all the more
the Church must cry:

"MERCY!"
Everything said in this encyclical
must be continually transformed
into an ardent prayer for mercy
for all of mankind,
even if the world deserves
another "flood,"
as in the time of Noah.

Let us appeal to God
through Christ,
mindful of the words of
Mary's Magnificat
which proclaims:
"Mercy ... from age to age;"
let us cry out
to the God of Mercy Himself
for this present generation!
Let us offer our cry
with Christ on the Cross:
"Father, forgive them."
Let us offer our cry
for the love of God
and for the love of man.

May the love of the Father
be revealed again
by the work of the Son
and the Holy Spirit.
May that love be shown
to be present
in the modern world
and to be more powerful
than evil, sin and death.
We pray through the intercession of Mary
Who does not cease to proclaim:
"Mercy ... from generation to generation." (15)

Chapter 2: Homilies and Addresses on Divine Mercy

Pope John Paul II has placed a strong emphasis on the Divine Mercy throughout his pontificate. Repeatedly he has written and spoken about the need for us to turn to the mercy of God as *the* answer to the specific problems of our times. The following excerpts are especially powerful and show *how* urgent he feels the message of Divine Mercy is for the world now, in our present human condition.

April 6, 1986, words of the Holy Father, Pope John Paul II addressed to pilgrims in St. Peter's Square, Rome at the noon-day recitation of the Regina Caeli:

I direct now my affectionate greeting to all the groups of pilgrims present in St. Peter's Square; in particular, I express a cordial welcome to the group of Roman supporters of The Divine Mercy, according to the message of Sister Faustina Kowalska, who celebrate today the feast of The Divine Mercy.

In a series of talks from 1981 to 1997 John Paul II spoke of the need to experience Divine Mercy in order to "be merciful just as your Father is merciful" (Lk. 6:36). For example, on November 22, 1981, Feast of Christ the King, Pope John Paul II made his first public visit outside of Rome following a lengthy recuperation from his bullet wounds, to the Shrine of Merciful Love in Collevalenza near Todi, Italy, where, within a few days, an international congress was to be held to reflect on the Encyclical *Dives in Misericordia* (*Rich in Mercy*) one year after is publication. After celebrating the Holy Sacrifice of the Eucharist, he made a strong public declaration about the importance of the message of mercy :

A year ago I published the encyclical *Dives in Misericordia.* This circumstance made me come to the Sanctuary of Merciful Love today. By my presence I wish to reconfirm, in a way, the message of that encyclical. I wish to read it again and deliver it again.

Right from the beginning of my ministry in St. Peter's See in Rome, I considered this message my special task. Providence has assigned it to me in the present situation of man, the Church and the world. It could be said that precisely this situation assigned that message to me as my task before God".

Then in a series of addresses on *Divine Mercy Sunday* over the years he continued to call us to the experience of God's mercy:[1]

• **April 10, 1991:** Pope John Paul II spoke about Sister Faustina, showing his great respect for her, relating her to his encyclical, *Rich in Mercy*, and emphasizing her role in bringing the message of mercy to the world:

The words of the encyclical on Divine Mercy (Dives in Misericordia) are particularly close to us. They recall the figure of the Servant of God, Sister Faustina Kowalska. This simple woman religious particularly brought the Easter message of the merciful Christ closer to Poland and the whole world... .

And today? ... Is it perhaps not necessary to translate into the language of today's generations the words of the Gospel, 'Blessed are the merciful, for they shall obtain mercy' (Mt. 5:7)?

• **April 18, 1993:** Sister Faustina was beatified by Pope John Paul II in Rome on the Second Sunday of Easter, which Our Lord had revealed to her as the "Feast of Mercy":

'I clearly feel that my mission does not end with death, but begins,' Sister Faustina wrote in her diary. And it truly did! Her mission continues and is yielding astonishing fruit. It is truly marvelous how her devotion to the merciful Jesus is spreading in our contemporary world and gaining so many human hearts! This is doubtlessly a sign of the times – a sign of our 20th century. The balance of this century

---

[1] For the text of the addresses at the Regina Caeli see the Appendix.

which is now ending, in addition to the advances which have often surpassed those of preceding eras, presents a deep restlessness and fear of the future. Where, if not in The Divine Mercy, can the world find refuge and the light of hope? Believers understand that perfectly.

Give thanks to the Lord, for He is good. Give thanks to the Lord, for He is merciful.

• **April 10, 1994:** Second Sunday of Easter, *Regina Caeli* Address:

What is mercy if not the boundless love of God, who confronted with human sin, restrains the sentiment of severe justice and, allowing Himself to be moved by the wretchedness of His creatures, spurs Himself to the total gift of self, in the Son's cross? 'O happy fault... which gained for us so great a Redeemer!' (Easter Proclamation).

Who can say he is free from sin and does not need God's mercy? As people of this restless time of ours, wavering between the emptiness of self-exaltation and the humiliation of despair, **we have a greater need than ever for a regenerating experience of mercy** (April 10, 1994, emphasis added).

In this address, John Paul II made a strong appeal for an *experience of mercy* that is regenerating. This means we need a revival of God's life within us. Then in the following year, again on Mercy Sunday, he made another strong appeal to all people to *personally* experience the tender mercy of the Father:

• **April 23, 1995:** Pope John Paul II celebrated Divine Mercy Sunday in Holy Spirit Church, the Shrine of Divine Mercy in Rome. (*L'Osservatore Romano*, English Edition, April 26, 1995). In his homily he challenged us to "trust in the Lord and be Apostles of Divine Mercy."

Sr. Faustina Kowalska's mystical experiences were all focused on the mystery of the merciful Christ .... [Her] mystical experience and her cry to the merciful Christ belong to the harsh context of our century's history. As people of this century which is now coming to an end, *we would like to thank the Lord for the message of Divine Mercy* (emphasis in the text) .... I would like to say to all: trust in the Lord! Be apostles of Divine Mercy and, following the invitation and example of Blessed Faustina, take care of those who suffer in body and especially in spirit. Let each one feel the merciful love of the Lord who comforts and instills joy.

In his *Regina Caeli* address, he spoke of this Octave of Easter as one day and this Sunday as the day of thanksgiving for God's mercy, called the Sunday of Divine Mercy:

Dear brothers and sisters, We must *personally experience* this [tender-hearted mercy of the Father] if, in turn, we want to be capable of mercy. *Let us learn to forgive!* The spiral of hatred and violence which stains with blood the path of so many individuals and nations can only be broken by the *miracle of forgiveness.* (italics in the text)

Here we have one of the great exhortations of the Mercy Pope calling us to personally experience the mercy of God that revives us and makes it possible for us to forgive.

The Personal Experience of the Mercy Pope

- **June 7, 1997:**

At the Shrine of Divine Mercy in Lagiewniki, outside of Krakow, Poland, where the relics of Sister Faustina are kept, John Paul II addressed the Sisters of Our Lady of Mercy. It was a personal testimony of his own involvement with the message of Divine Mercy and a sweeping summary of both the message and devotion to The Divine Mercy.

The following excerpts highlight the Pope's personal experience of Divine Mercy:

Purpose of his pilgrimage: "I have come here 'to sing of the mercies of the Lord forever'" (Ps 89:2).

Urgency: "There is nothing that mankind needs more than Divine Mercy."

The Message: Divine Mercy is "that love which is benevolent, which is compassionate, which raises man above his weakness to the infinite heights of the holiness of God."

The Image: "Those who gaze on the image of the merciful Jesus hear, like Blessed Faustina, 'Fear nothing, I am with you.'"

Trust: "Those who sincerely say 'Jesus, I trust in You' will find comfort in all their anxieties and fears."

The Church: regards the message of Divine Mercy as "the light of hope" and "unceasingly implores mercy for all".

Commends: "the concerns of the Church and humanity to the merciful Christ."

Entrusts to the Divine Mercy: "once more [his] Petrine ministry, 'Jezu Ufam Tobie!' [Jesus, I trust in You!]."

Personal Witness: "The message of Divine Mercy has always been near and dear to me."

Pontificate: "I took with me [the message of Divine Mercy] to the See of Peter and which in a sense *forms the image of this Pontificate*" (emphasis added).

Divine Mercy Sunday: "I give thanks to divine Providence that I have been enabled to contribute personally to the fulfillment of Christ's will through the institution of the *Feast of Divine Mercy*" [in Poland] (emphasis added).

Chaplet of The Divine Mercy: "I pray unceasingly that God will 'have mercy on us and on the whole world'" (Chaplet).

Challenge to the Sisters of Our Lady of Mercy: "Accept the responsibility of your extraordinary vocation! The people of today need your *proclamation* of Divine Mercy, your *works* of mercy, and your *prayer* for mercy."

Prayer for all: "May The Divine Mercy transform hearts. ... we all need it so much as the third millennium approaches."

"I cordially bless all those devoted to The Divine Mercy."

NOTE: See the Appendix for the full text.

• **April 19, 1998:** Again on Divine Mercy Sunday, the Mercy Pope calls us to "accept Divine Mercy with an open heart".

• **April 11, 1999:** John Paul II called the Octave Day of Easter Divine Mercy Sunday. He encouraged all to be apostles of Divine Mercy like Blessed Faustina. He invited us to intensify our prayer for peace as a gift of mercy.

Cardinal Fiorenzo Angelini celebrated Divine Mercy Sunday in St. Peter's Square with some 30,000 faithful from around the world.

• **April 30, 2000:** Before some 250,000 pilgrims and the television cameras of the world, Pope John Paul II canonized Sr. Faustina Kowalska, "the great Apostle of Divine Mercy". In this way, he also "canonized" the Divine Mercy message and devotion, and also declared the Second Sunday of Easter as "Divine Mercy Sunday" for the universal Church:

It is important that we *accept the whole message* that comes to us from the Word of God on this Second Sunday of Easter, which from now on throughout the Church will be called "Divine Mercy Sunday." (*Divine Mercy Sunday*, April 30, 2000)

In one of the most extraordinary homilies of his pontificate, Pope John Paul II repeated three times that Sr. Faustina is "God's gift to our time". She made the message of Divine Mercy the "bridge to the third millennium". He then said:

By this act of canonization of Sr. Faustina, I intend today to pass this message on to the third millennium. I pass it on to all people, so that they will learn to know even better the true face of God and the true face of their neighbor. In fact, love of God and love of one's neighbor are inseparable.

He exhorted all of us to join our voices to Mary, Mother of Mercy, and Saint Faustina "who made her life a hymn to mercy" and "sing the mercies of the Lord forever" (Ps 89:2).

He further exhorted us to make her prayer of trustful abandonment our own and say with firm hope:

Jesus I trust in You!

Chapter 3:   Divine Mercy in Various Writings

Redeemer of Man (*Redemptor Hominis*), March 4, 1979

In the opening line of his first encyclical, John Paul II proclaims:

The Redeemer of Man, Jesus Christ, is the center of the universe and of history (#1).

... Through the Incarnation God gave human life the dimension that He intended man to have from his first beginning; He has granted that dimension definitively – in the way that is peculiar to Him alone, in keeping with His *eternal love and mercy* (#1).

Then in the chapter on the *Mystery* of the *Redemption*, John Paul II describes the great gift of love that is also described as *mercy* which is a person: *Jesus Christ:*

Therefore "for our sake (God) made Him (the Son) to be sin who knew no sin." If He "made to be sin" Him who was without any sin whatever, it was to reveal the love that is always greater than the whole of creation, the love that is He, Himself, since "God is love". Above all, love is greater than sin, than weakness, than the "futility of creation"; it is stronger than death; it is a love always ready to raise up and forgive, always ready to go to meet the prodigal son; always looking for "the revealing of the sons of God", who are called to the glory that is to be revealed. *This revelation of love is also described as mercy; and in man's history this revelation of love and mercy has taken a form and a name: that of Jesus Christ* (emphasis added #9).

This revelation of mercy is further developed in John Paul II's second encyclical *Rich in Mercy* as *Mercy Incarnate:* Jesus Christ. He uses as a repeated theme: Mercy, love's second name, is more powerful than evil, more powerful than sin and death.

In *Redeemer of Man* John Paul II first develops the mystic sense of the "new Advent", the exhortation "Do not be afraid!" and the need of imploring God's mercy (see later chapters).

Lord and Giver of Life (*Dominum et Vivificatem*) Encyclical on the Holy Spirit in the Life of the Church and world (Pentecost, May 18, 1986)

In the third encyclical of the trilogy, John Paul II opens with a description of the Holy Spirit in terms of the "Law of the Gift:"

> The Church professes her faith in the Holy Spirit as *"the Lord, the giver of life."*

In section #39, John Paul II describes the Holy Spirit as Spirit-love who transforms suffering into salvific love – mercy personified:

> The Holy Spirit, who is the love of the Father and the Son ... is the source of every divine giving of gifts to creatures. Precisely in Him we can picture as personified and actualized in a transcendent way that mercy which the Patristic and theological tradition, following the line of the Old and New Testaments, attributes to God. In man, mercy includes sorrow and compassion for the misfortunes of one's neighbor. In God, the Spirit-love expresses the consideration of human sin in a fresh outpouring of salvific love.(#39)

The Holy Spirit is not only the Giver of Life, Spirit-love, He is also mercy personified! He is salvific love.

Mission of the Redeemer (*Redemptoris Missio*) December 7, 1990

The theme of this encyclical is the urgency of missionary activity based on the mission of the Holy Trinity (see #1). The one purpose of renewed missionary commitment is to serve man by revealing to him the love of God manifest in Jesus Christ (#2). Christ is the revelation and incarnation of the Father's mercy (#12). Christ makes the kingdom of God present and inaugurates the kingdom of the Father's love and compassion. All are invited to repent and believe in God's merciful love (#13).

Gospel of Life (*Evangelium Vitae*), March 25, 1995:

In his encyclical *Evangelium Vitae,* John Paul II begins with a statement on the Gospel of mercy. He states that Jesus, Mercy Incarnate, reveals the Good News that God's love is life-giving:

> The Gospel of life is at the heart of Jesus' message (#1).

In dealing with the culture of death – with birth control, abortion, euthanasia, suicide – he proclaims the Gospel of life – Jesus!:

> Jesus is the only Gospel. To proclaim Jesus is itself to proclaim life. ... This Gospel exceeds every human expectation and reveals the sublime heights to which the dignity of the human person is raised by grace (#80).

The Gospel of life is *mercy*: life-giving love and love-giving life:

> As part of the spiritual worship acceptable to God (cf. Rom 12:1), the Gospel of life is to be celebrated above all in daily living, which should be filled with self-giving love for others. In this way, our lives will become a genuine and responsible acceptance of the gift of life and a heartfelt song of praise and gratitude to God, who has given us this gift. This is already happening in the many different acts of selfless generosity, often humble and hidden, carried out by men and women, children and adults, the young and the old, the healthy and the sick.

It is in this context, so humanly rich and filled with love, that *heroic actions* too are born. These are the most solemn celebration of the Gospel of life, for they proclaim it by the total gift of self. They are the radiant manifestation of the highest degree of love, which is *to give one's life for the person loved* (cf Jn 15:13). They are a sharing in the mystery of the cross, in which Jesus reveals the *value of every person and how life attains its fullness in the sincere gift of self.* (#86)

The Gospel of life is not for believers alone: It is for everyone (#101).

It is precisely in the *flesh* of every person that Christ continues to reveal himself and to enter into fellowship with us, so that the rejection of human life, in whatever form that rejection takes, is really a rejection of Christ (#104).

Life is a gift of God's mercy, John Paul II teaches to all. A rejection of life is a rejection of God Himself.

Gift and Mystery: on the Fiftieth Anniversary of my Priestly Ordination, November 1, 1946-1996

Pope John Paul II writes his memoirs:

I recall these things above all in order to thank the Lord. "I will sing of the mercies of the Lord forever" (Ps 89:2). I offer this to priests and to the people of God as a testimony of love [Introduction].

The priest is a minister of mercy ... The witness and instrument of Divine Mercy ... It is in the confessional that every priest becomes a witness of the great miracles Divine Mercy works in souls which receive the grace of conversion (p. 86).

The Day of the Lord (*Dies Domini*), Apostolic Letter, May 31, 1998

John Paul II described the weekly Sunday celebration of the

Holy Eucharist as the "weekly Easter" and the "weekly Pentecost." Now that he has declared the Second Sunday of Easter as "Divine Mercy Sunday," the prime eighth day becomes a "weekly Divine Mercy celebration." The Gospel of the Easter night appearance is used in both Mercy Sunday and Pentecost.

Part II: Model of Mercy

John Paul II not only teaches about mercy, he puts his teaching into practice: by praying for mercy; by forgiving and asking for forgiveness; by radiating mercy; by his presence; by ministry to the sick, the suffering and the poor.

Chapter 4:   Prayer for Mercy

On November 11, 1986, I had the privilege of concelebrating Holy Mass with the Holy Father in his private chapel. We entered the chapel at 6:45 am for the 7:00 Mass. John Paul was deep in prayer, kneeling with his face in his hands. I was seated a yard from him. For that quarter of an hour I wondered what he was praying. What came to me was that he was praying: "Jesus, Mercy!"

It was years later that he said at the Shrine of Divine Mercy in Poland, June 7, 1997, that "I pray unceasingly that God will have 'mercy on us and on the whole world'" (Chaplet of Divine Mercy).

John Paul II shared his call for prayer for mercy at the conclusion of his encyclical on Divine Mercy :

The Church Appeals to the Mercy of God[2]

The Church proclaims the truth about God's mercy which is

[2] From a new translation of the encyclical Rich in Mercy. The original Polish text, written in longhand by Pope John Paul II in his native tongue flows ever so smoothly, using words that are delicately and specifically chosen. The Latin and English translations, which had to be done quickly and immediately for the Vatican Polyglot Press do not convey the full strength and beauty of the original text.

The intention of this translation, using the original Polish as well as the English and Latin Vatican Polyglot Press translations as a basis, is to convey the spiritual power of the message. There are a number of factors that would need to be combined to do this with the greatest force: a knowledge of Polish, an ease with the existential philosophical mode of thinking of John Paul II, a thorough grasp of his message of mercy and the origins of his concern about mercy, and a knowledge of the English language. I cannot claim expertise in all of the above needed factors, but I am very much aware of the urgency of the message of mercy and the origins of the concern of Pope John Paul. May my inadequacy in Polish and English, and my weakness in existential philosophy be overcome by my burning desire to convey the Holy Father's message of mercy.

I tried to bring out the force of the Pope's message by using the English phrases and words that seemed to be as strong as his words. The changes made most often involved an addition of the phrase or word referred to in a reflective pronoun. Often, the sentences or paragraphs in the Official English translation were so long that the "it" became ambiguous and the sentence lost its force. This repeating of the subject makes the sentences clear and strong. Some sentences were divided in order to convey the full impact of the message.

made known in the crucified and risen Christ and she makes it known in various ways. The Church also tries to be merciful to people through people because she considers this to be an indispensable condition for a better, "more human" world, today and tomorrow.

And yet at no time and in no period of history – especially at a turning point like ours – can the Church forget about *prayer, which is a cry for the mercy of God* in the midst of the many forms of evil that weigh upon mankind and threaten it. This imploring of mercy is precisely the fundamental right and at the same time the duty of the Church in Christ Jesus. It is the right and duty of the Church toward God and at the same time toward humanity.

The more the human conscience succumbs to secularization and loses its sense of the very meaning of the word "mercy," the more it moves away from God and the mystery of mercy. Therefore *the Church has all the more the right and the duty* to appeal to God's mercy with "loud cries" (Heb 5:7). Such "loud cries" ought to be the cry of the Church of our times to God for mercy as she announces and proclaims the certainty of that mercy in the crucified and risen Christ, that is, the Paschal Mystery. This mystery carries within itself the fullest revelation of mercy, namely, that love is more powerful than death, more powerful than sin and every evil, that love lifts man from his deepest falls and frees him from his greatest threats.

Modern man feels these threats. What has been said on this point is only a beginning. Modern man often asks about the solutions of these terrible tensions which have built up in the world between peoples. And if at times he *lacks the courage to utter this word "mercy,"* or if his conscience is empty of religious content and he does not find the equivalent, so much greater is the *necessity for the Church to utter this word,* not only in her own name but also in the name of all people of our time.

It is necessary that everything that I have said in this present letter on mercy *be continuously changed and transformed into an ardent prayer:* into a cry for mercy on the people of the modern world with all their needs and threats. *May this cry be filled with that truth about mercy* which has found such rich expression in the Sacred Scriptures, in Tradition, and in the authentic life of faith of countless generations of the People of God. Like the sacred writers, let us cry out to God who cannot despise anything that He has made, (Gen 1:31; Ps 145:9; Wis 11:24), to Him who is faithful to Himself, His fatherhood and His love. And like the prophets, let us appeal to that love which has maternal characteristics – and, like a mother, goes after each of her children, after each lost sheep, even if the lost are in the millions, even if the evil in the world outweighs honesty, even if mankind deserves, because of its sins, a kind of modern "flood," as did the generation of Noah.

Let us then appeal also to that kind of fatherly love revealed to us by Christ in His messianic mission, which reached its ultimate expression in His cross, in His death and in His resurrection! Let us appeal to God through Christ, mindful of the words of Mary's *Magnificat* which proclaims "mercy from age to age". Let us cry out for God's own mercy for this present generation! May the Church which, like Mary, continues to be the spiritual mother of humankind, express in this prayer her total maternal concern, as well as that trusting love from which is born the most burning need for prayer.

Let us cry out, guided by that faith, hope and love that Christ grafted in our hearts. This cry for mercy is at the same time an expression of our love of God, from whom modern man has distanced himself and made of Him a stranger, proclaiming in various ways that he doesn't "need" God. This then is mercy, the *love of God* whose insult – rejection by modern man – we feel deeply and are ready to cry out with Christ on the cross, "Father, forgive them, for they do not know what they do" (Lk 23:34 RSV).

This cry for mercy is at the same time love for all of mankind. Mercy is love for all peoples without exception or division: without difference of race, culture, language, or world-view, without distinction between friends and enemies. This cry for mercy is love for all people. Mercy desires every true good for each individual and for every human community, for every family, for every nation, for every social group, for youth, adults, parents, and for the elderly and the sick. It is love for everyone, without exception or division. This cry for mercy is love for all people, the care which ensures for everyone all true good, and removes and drives away every sort of evil.

And if any of our contemporaries do not share the faith and hope which bid me, as servant of the mysteries of God (cf 1 Cor 1:1), to implore the mercy of God Himself for mankind in this hour of history, *then may they understand the reason for my concern. It is dictated by love* for mankind, for all that is human and which, according to the intuitions of many of our contemporaries, is threatened by an immense danger.

The same mystery of Christ, which reveals to us the great vocation of mankind, which obliged me to proclaim in the Encyclical *Redemptor Hominis* mankind's incomparable dignity, also obliges me to announce mercy as God's merciful love revealed in that same mystery of Christ. This mystery of Christ also obliges me to appeal to this mercy and implore this mercy on our difficult and critical times of the Church and of the world as we approach the end of the second millennium.

In the name of Jesus Christ crucified and risen from the dead, in the spirit of His messianic mission, which endures in the works of mankind, *we lift up our voice and plead:* that the love which is in the Father, may once again be revealed at this stage of history; and that, through the work of the Son and the Holy Spirit, this love which is in the Father, may be once again shown to be present in our modern world as more powerful than evil and more powerful than sin and death. We plead this through the intercession of Mary, who does not cease to proclaim "mercy ... from generation to generation," and also through the intercession of the saints in whom have been completely fulfilled the words of the Sermon on the Mount: "Blessed are the merciful, for they shall obtain mercy": (Mt 5:7).

It is not permissible for the Church, for any reason, to withdraw into herself as she continues the great task of implementing the Second Vatican Council. In this implementing we can rightly see a new phase of the self-realization of the Church – in keeping with the age in which it has been our destiny to live. *The reason for her existence* is, in fact, to reveal God, that Father who allows us to "see" Himself in Christ (cf Jn 14:9). No matter how strong the resistance of human history may be, no matter how estranged the civilization of the world, no matter how great the denial of God in the human world, so much the greater must be our closeness to that mystery which, hidden for centuries in God, was then truly shared with man, in time, through Jesus Christ.

Chapter 5:   Forgiving and asking for forgiveness

Forgiveness is the first act of mercy. *The Catechism of the Catholic Church* teaches the centrality of forgiveness when explaining the conditional phrase of the Lord's prayer: "Forgive us our trespasses as we forgive those who trespass against us" (C.C.C. #2838 to 2845). This section is one of the most extraordinary teachings in the catechism.

Sacred Scripture teaches us that "Our redemption is the forgiveness of sins" (Col 1:14). And in St. Paul's letter to Titus (3:5) we read:

When the kindness and love of God our Savior appeared, He saved us; not because of any righteous deeds we have done, but because of His mercy.

John Paul II in his encyclical, *Rich in Mercy* points out the source of the mercy we need in order to be merciful and forgive; namely, Christ crucified:

Christ's messianic program, the program of mercy, becomes the program of His people, the program of the Church. At its very center there is always the cross, for it is in the cross that the revelation of merciful love attains its culmination. (#8)

And further he points to the Heart of Jesus as the center:

The Church seems in a special way to profess the mercy of God and to venerate it when she directs herself to the Heart of Christ. In fact, it is precisely this drawing close to Christ in the mystery of His Heart which enables us to dwell on this point ... of the revelation which constituted the central content of the messianic mission of the Son of Man. (#13)

John Paul II in sections #12 and #14 develops the relationship of mercy, forgiveness and justice. As we shall point out, forgiveness is a major *modus operandi* for him in the present world condition. After developing the lack of peace and the threat of destruction which is linked with the very existence of humanity (#11), he asks the question: "Is Justice Enough?" "Justice alone is not enough" (#12). Mercy, "that deeper power, which is love, must shape human life in its various dimensions – otherwise the highest justice is the greatest injury" (see #12).

In section #14 John Paul II points out that the "Church must acknowledge as her principal duty – at every stage of history and especially in our modern age – *to proclaim and to introduce into life* the mystery of mercy. ... It is precisely in the name of this mystery that Christ teaches us to forgive always:"

It is important, John Paul II points out, that:

Forgiveness does not cancel out the objective requirements of justice. ... Properly understood, justice constitutes the goal of forgiveness. ... Mercy has the power to confer on justice a new content, which is expressed most simply in forgiveness (#14).

Then he summarizes the mission of the Church in terms of forgiveness:

The Church rightly considers it her duty and purpose of her mission to guard the authenticity of forgiveness ... by guarding its *source* which is the mystery of the mercy of God himself as revealed in Jesus Christ. ... The basis of the Church's mission is none other than 'drawing from the wells of the Savior' (Is 12:3) (#14).

The Pope Asks Forgiveness

One of the characteristics of the Mercy Pope is to express the mission of the Church in concrete terms by asking for forgiveness.

In *Tertio Millennium Adveniente* (November 10, 1994) John Paul II prays that unity among all Christians will increase until they reach full communion – as soon as possible (#16). The jubilee preparation should make the Church more fully conscious of our sinfulness, especially of scandal and counter- witness (#33). We must repent of sins against unity. We must make amends and teach forgiveness. We should invoke the Holy Spirit with greater insistence for the grace of Christian unity (#34). The Church must express profound regret for intolerance and violence in the service of truth (#35).

John Paul II has done this in his meetings with Protestant groups, for example, with the Protestants in the Czech Republic. In *Orientale Lumen* (May 2, 1995) he says that we must ceaselessly implore Divine Mercy and a new heart for a shared conversion (#21).

In his encyclical *Ut Unum Sint* (May 25, 1995) he writes that what is needed is "a vision enlivened by Divine Mercy" to break down walls of division and distrust:

> The commitment to ecumenism must be based upon conversion of hearts and upon prayer, which will lead to the necessary purification of past memories. With the grace of the Holy Spirit, the Lord's disciples, inspired by love, by the power of the truth and a sincere desire for mutual forgiveness and reconciliation are called to *re-examine together their painful past ... What is needed is ...* a vision enlivened by Divine Mercy. (#2)

John Paul II writes strongly of his ministry as bishop of Rome as a ministry of mercy, even as Peter received mercy to, in turn, minister mercy to his brethren (cf Jn 22:32):

> "The Bishop of Rome exercises a ministry originating in the manifold mercy of God. This mercy converts hearts ... and is completely at the service of God's merciful plan (#92) ... [He] knows that he must be a sign of mercy. His is a ministry of mercy, born of an act of Christ's own mercy. ... God in his mercy can convert hearts to unity and enable them to enter into communion with him (#93). This service of unity, rooted in the action of Divine Mercy, is

entrusted within the College of Bishops. ... This task can require the offering of one's own life" (cf Jn 10: 11-18) (#94).

In addition to his encyclicals, John Paul II has expressed mercy by asking forgiveness from various groups for the lack of mercy they have experienced from the Catholic Church over the course of history. In addition to the Eastern Churches and various Protestant groups, he has asked forgiveness of those who experienced injustice and lack of understanding in the Inquisition. He also asked forgiveness of Jewish groups for the persecution they experienced, and from scientists because of the condemnation of Galileo. In a moving encounter, he forgave Ali Agca, the man who shot him and caused him months of pain. (See *When a Pope Asks Forgiveness, The Mea Culpas of John Paul II,* by Luigi Accattoli, Pauline Books and Media, 1998). In June, 2000, Pope John Paul II expressed his pleasure with the Italian government's decision to grant clemency to his would-be assassin.

In *Incarnationis Mysterium*, November 29, 1998, John Paul II officially proclaimed the Jubilee Year of the Year 2000. In a beautiful way he described the year of Jubilee as the "Year of Mercy." He asked the Church to exercise the mercy she had received from the Lord by kneeling before God and imploring forgiveness for the past and present sins of her sons and daughters (#11). He prayed that the year would be *"an especially deep experience of grace and Divine Mercy"* (#6). Once again he wrote of the mercy of God as a sign of the charity that is needed to reduce or even forgive the debt of the poorer nations, presented earlier in *Tertio Millenio Adveniente* (#51):

> Some nations, especially the poorer ones, are oppressed by a debt so high that repayment is impossible. ... The abuses of power which result in some dominating others must stop: Such abuses are sinful and unjust (#12).

In one of the highlights of the Jubilee Year of Mercy, on

March 12, 2000, Pope John Paul II, along with seven cardinals who were heads of Vatican Congregations, solemnly asked God for forgiveness for a number of past and present actions of the sons and daughters of the Church. They prayed in turn a confession of sins, asking for forgiveness (See Appendix for the full text):

I.   Sins in general.

II.   Sins committed in the service of truth.

III.   Sins which have harmed the unity of the Body of Christ.

IV.   Sins against the people of Israel.

V.   Sins committed in actions against love, peace, the rights of peoples, and respect for cultures and religions.

VI.   Confession of sins against the dignity of women and the unity of the human race.

VII.   Sins in relation to the fundamental rights of persons.

In the Angelus message following Mass, Pope John Paul II said:

As we ask for forgiveness, we forgive. This is what we say every day when we pray the prayer Christ taught us: "Our Father ... forgive us our trespasses as we forgive those who trespass against us" (Full text in the Appendix).

Chapter 6: Radiating presence: Holiness

John Paul II radiates God's presence. He electrifies people when he greets them individually or in massive crowds. People are converted by his very presence.

St. Faustina recorded the words of our Lord about the radiation of His mercy:

I am Love and Mercy itself. When a soul approaches Me with trust, I fill it with such an abundance of graces that it cannot contain them within itself, *but radiates them to other souls* (Diary, 1074).

St. Faustina prayed for this radiation of mercy:

I want to be completely transformed into Your mercy and to be Your living reflection, O Lord. May the greatest of all divine attributes, that of Your unfathomable mercy, pass through my heart and soul to my neighbor (Diary, 163).

John Paul II is a holy man who entrusted his pontificate to The Divine Mercy: "Jesus, I trust in You!" and Divine Mercy "forms the image of [his] pontificate" (Shrine of Divine Mercy, Poland, June 7, 1997). He is totally abandoned to the truth of the living Word of God (see *Mother of the Redeemer* #14), and, like Mary, totally entrusted to the will of God: "Totus Tuus." In short, John Paul II is a holy man, a man of God, a man who prays.

We can understand John Paul II better from the answer Father Adam Boniecki, M.I.C., (past editor of the Polish edition of *L'Osservatore Romano* and personal friend of the Pope) gave to a question about the personal life of John Paul II: "Why don't you write about the personal life of the Pope? For example, what does he like for breakfast? What does he do to relax?"

Father Adam answered, "I did write an article about the Pope's daily life which the Pope okayed. But, he lives the life of a Carmelite. He is either working or praying!"

John Paul II's dedication to prayer and to the work of the Lord is so evident that mercy radiates out from him.

Chapter 7:   Ministry to the sick and poor

John Paul II responds with mercy to the sick. He established a yearly celebration, *The World Day of the Sick,* (February 11, the Feast of Our Lady of Lourdes).

On February 11, 1989, I personally saw his compassion for the sick as he laid hands of blessing upon each of the hundreds of sick in wheelchairs and stretchers assembled in St. Peter's Basilica.

In the encyclical, *Gospel of Life*, May 13, 1993, John Paul II wrote:

Pain and suffering have meaning and value when they are experienced in close connection with love received and given. In this regard I have called for the yearly celebration of the *World Day of the Sick*, [February 11], emphasizing the salvific nature of offering up of suffering which, experienced in communion with Christ, belongs to the very essence of the redemption (#94).

In the Apostolic Letter, *On the Christian Meaning of Human Suffering (Salvifici Dolores)*, February 11, 1984, John Paul II describes how Jesus Christ transforms suffering into salvific love. Moreover, He has opened His salvific suffering to man. He lives in the one He has loved by suffering and dying (#20). "At one and the same time Christ has taught man *to do good by his suffering and to do good to those who suffer.* He has completely revealed the meaning of suffering (#30).

In his conclusion, John Paul II prayed that all peoples of all times might find in the Redeemer, the Man of Sorrows who has taken on all our physical and moral sufferings, the love that gives salvific meaning to their sorrows. He asked all who suffer to support him. "May your suffering in union with the cross of Christ be victorious!" (#31)

In his pilgrimages around the world, John Paul II has visited the ghettoes, the poorest of the poor and the native peoples. His very presence is a sign of hope and encouragement.

Part III: Mercy Themes

Repeated themes in the writings and teachings of John Paul II, like repeated themes in a symphony, express his compassion and love for God and for all human beings.

Chapter 8:   The value and dignity of each person

Throughout his teachings and writings we hear the repeated theme of the dignity, the meaning and the value of each person, stressing the right to freedom of every human being. This repeated theme is an expression of his existential phenomenology, a philosophy that focuses on the subjective response to objective reality. It is a form of personalism that stresses the fact that we are created in the image and likeness of God (Genesis 1:26-27). This text of Genesis is the foundation of his moral ethic: since we are created in the image of God we are to behave like God.

John Paul II has repeated often the text of the Vatican II document on the Church and the modern world (*Gaudium et spes*, #22) that:

Christ, the new Adam, in the very revelation of the mystery of the Father and his love, *fully reveals man to himself and brings to light his most high calling* (quoted in *Redeemer of Man*, #8).

In the same encyclical he deals with the Church's mission and human freedom quoting the Vatican II document on Human Freedom:

The missionary attitude always begins with a feeling of deep esteem for "what is in man" (Declaration *Nostra Aetate*, 1-2).

This theme of human dignity, developed more fully in the second encyclical of John Paul II, *Rich in Mercy,* is found in the parable of the prodigal son (#5-6):

The inheritance that the son has received from his father was a quantity of material goods, but more important than the goods was *his dignity as a son in his father's house* (#5). ... The father's fidelity to himself is totally concentrated upon the humanity of the lost son, upon his dignity (#6). ... The relationship of mercy is based on the common experience of the dignity that is proper to him (#6). ... Mercy is manifested in its true and proper aspect when it restores to value, promotes and draws good from all the forms of evil existing in the world and in man (#6).

The Catechism of the Catholic Church develops the theme of the *Dignity of the Human Person* (# 1700-1876) in an extensive way quoting Sacred Scripture, the Church Fathers, the Vatican II document on the Church and the modern world (*Gaudium et Spes*), and the writings of John Paul II. This theme of the dignity of man is also developed in the sections on creation (355-421), on the sixth commandment (2331-2400), and the sacrament of marriage (400-414).

The theme of the dignity, freedom, and equality of man is strongly developed in John Paul II's *Theology of the Body* (Wednesday elocutions from 1979 to 1984) developing his teaching on sexuality, marriage and celibacy as an expression of the "Law of the Gift." Christopher West beautifully summarizes John Paul II's *Theology of the Body* (*Inside the Vatican*, November 1998, p.42 ff.).

Chapter 9:   Be not afraid

John Paul II began his papacy with the cry: "Be not afraid!"

When, on October 22, 1978, I said the words "Be not afraid!" in St. Peter's Square, I could not fully know how far they would take me and the entire Church. Their meaning came more from the Holy Spirit, the Consoler, promised by the Lord Jesus to His disciples, than from the man who spoke them. Nevertheless, with the passing of the years, I have recalled these words on many occasions. ... Why should we have no fear? Because man has been redeemed by God. ... The power of Christ's Cross and Resurrection is greater than any evil which man could or should fear (*Threshold of Hope*, 1994).

On one special occasion he recalled these words, "Be not afraid" while at the Shrine of Divine Mercy in Poland, June 7, 1997. He related them to the abandonment of self-giving that is the "Law of the Gift" in the message of Divine Mercy:

And it is a *message that is clear and understandable for everyone.* Anyone can come here, look at this image of the merciful Jesus, His Heart radiating grace, and hear in the depths of his own soul what Blessed Faustina heard: *"Fear nothing. I am with you always"* (Diary, 586).

And if this person responds with a sincere heart: *"Jesus, I trust in you,"* he will find comfort in all his *anxieties and fears.* In this "dialogue of abandonment," there is established between man and Christ a *special bond that sets love free.* And "there is no fear in love, but perfect love casts out fear" (1 Jn 4:18).

John Paul II relates his "Be not afraid" theme to *trust in Jesus.* He then goes on to renew once more his entrustment of his Petrine pontificate to the merciful Lord by praying: "Jesus I trust in You!"

At the Canonization of St. Faustina, John Paul II again related the prayer "Jesus, I trust in You!" to his theme of "Be not afraid:"

> This simple act of abandonment to Jesus dispels the thickest of clouds and lets a ray of light penetrate every life. Jezu, ufam Tobie (#8).

And addressing Faustina, he prayed as a conclusion to his homily:

> Fixing our gaze with you on the face of the risen Christ, let us make our own your prayer of trusting abandonment and say with firm hope: Christ "Jesus, I trust in you!" "Jezu, ufam Tobie!"

"Singing of the mercies of the Lord forever" (Ps 89.2) is another way John Paul II expresses his trust and hope that overcomes fear. He has repeated this "Singing of the mercies of the Lord forever" at the significant moments of his pontificate:

- *At Fatima,* May 13, 1982, a year after the attempted assassination, he came to give thanks to the Mother of Divine Mercy by "Singing of the mercies of the Lord" (Ps 89). In his parting address he said:

> "I began this pilgrimage with the canticle of God's mercy in my heart; and, on my departure, I want to tell you that my soul is still vibrating with this canticle; and 'I will sing the mercies of the Lord' (Ps 89) in the choir of the present generation of the Church, which has as first soloist the Mother of Divine Mercy."

- *On his 75th birthday,* May 18, 1995, he thanked God for the graces of his parents, his ordination as priest and bishop saying he is "singing the mercies of God forever!"

- *On his 50th anniversary of ordination,* November 1, 1996, he published his memoirs as priest recalling all these things as "singing of the mercies of the Lord forever!"

- *On coming to the Shrine of Divine Mercy in Poland,* June 7,

1997, he began his address with "'I will sing of the mercies of the Lord forever!' – and join the unending hymn in honor of Divine Mercy."

- Then at the *Canonization of St. Faustina,* April 30, 2000, he began with Psalm 118:1, "Give thanks to the Lord for He is good; his mercy endures forever." In his text he quoted Psalm 89, and stated that Sr. Faustina had made her life a hymn to mercy. Then again he said:

"The mercies of the Lord I will sing forever" (Ps 89). Let us too, the pilgrim Church, join our voice to the voice of Mary most holy, "Mother of Mercy" to the voice of the new saint who sings of mercy with all God's friends in heavenly Jerusalem."

Chapter 10:   The Call to Holiness, Evangelization and Ecumenism

John Paul II has focused on three areas of the Second Vatican Council and made them into themes of his pontificate: the universal call to holiness, a new evangelization and ecumenism that will lead to Church unity.

Universal Call to Holiness

In Chapter Five of the Dogmatic Constitution (*Lumen Gentium*) of Vatican II entitled: "The Call of the Whole Church to Holiness" we read:

In the Church, everyone belonging to the hierarchy, or being cared for by it, is called to holiness, according to the saying of the Apostle: "For this is the will of God, your sanctification" (1 Th 4:3; Eph 1:4).

Pope John Paul II has very actively encouraged us to sanctity, to union with Jesus Christ. From the beginning of his pontificate he has challenged us to "open our hearts to the Redeemer!"

Moreover, John Paul II has given us many models of holiness during his 22 years as Pope. He has beatified over 800 men and women, most of them martyrs for their faith in the Lord. St. Faustina was the 197th saint he canonized – there have been only 593 saints canonized in the last 500 years! John Paul II has certainly made it loud and clear that he wants us to follow their example. This world needs millions of saints to call down God's mercy!

New Evangelization

In the encyclical *Mission of the Redeemer* (*Redemptoris Missio*), 1990, John Paul II presents the third millennium as a time to reach out with the Good News of Jesus Christ to the nations and to those who need re-evangelization:

As the third millennium of redemption draws near, God is preparing a *great springtime for Christianity.* ... For each believer as for the entire Church, the missionary task must remain foremost, for it concerns the eternal destiny of humanity and corresponds to God's mysterious and merciful plan (# 18).

Everyone is called to evangelize – to tell others of *God's mysteries and merciful plan!*

And the first form of evangelization is *witness* (#42) of our own lives. The first proclamation of Christ is to proclaim His salvation in our own lives and the offering of salvation to all people "as a gift of God's grace and mercy."

St. Augustine loved to say that we must evangelize, and if necessary, use words!

Ecumenism: Commitment to Church Unity

"Promoting the restoration of unity among all Christians is one of the chief concerns of the Second Sacred Ecumenical Synod of the Vatican." The Decree on Ecumenism opens with this statement that John Paul II has carried out as a major thrust of his pontificate and his encyclical, *That they be One* (*Ut Unum Sint*), with the subtitle "On Commitment to Ecumenism."

John Paul II has reached out to Protestant and Orthodox groups around the world, calling for prayer, dialogue of our gifts (not just a dialogue of ideas), mutual forgiveness and conversion.

John Paul II has set his heart on the unity of the Church. How can the world believe our witness if those who confess the name of Christ are divided?

Chapter 11:   Mary, Mother of Mercy

Mary has been a central theme of John Paul II's pontificate. This is evident in his motto "Totus Tuus" – I am all yours Mary – and his repeated consecrations to Mary at various shrines around the world. He has concluded each of his encyclicals with a prayer to Mary.

• *Rich in Mercy (Dives in Misericordia),* has a special section on Mary, Mother of Mercy (#9). (See the Appendix for the full text):

Mary proclaimed on the threshold of her kinswoman's house: "His mercy is ... from generation to generation" (Lk 1:50). Mary is also the one who experienced mercy in a particular and exceptional way, as no other person has. At the same time, still in an exceptional way, she made possible with the sacrifice of her heart her own sharing in revealing God's mercy. This sacrifice is intimately linked with the Cross of her Son, at the foot of which she was to stand on Calvary. Her sacrifice is a unique sharing in the revelation of mercy.

• *Mother of the Redeemer (Redemptoris Mater),* Encyclical on the Blessed Virgin Mary in the Life of the Pilgrim Church, March 25, 1987.

John Paul II describes the faith of Mary and how she abandoned herself to the truth of the word of the living God (#14).

Mary shares in the great mystery of mercy:

Through this faith Mary is perfectly united with Christ in his self-emptying [the Law of the Gift in our redemption] ... At the foot of the Cross, Mary shares through faith in the shocking mystery of this self-emptying. This is perhaps the deepest *"Kenosis" of faith* in human history (#18).

As Virgin and Mother she was singularly united in His first coming, so through her continued collaboration with Him she will also be united with Him in the expectation of the second; ... she also has that specifically maternal role of *mediatrix of mercy* at His final coming (#41, emphasis added).

- *Gospel of Life (Evangelium Vitae)* March 25, 1995

John Paul II concludes his encyclical by entrusting the unborn babies to Mary with a prayer to proclaim the gospel of life:

> O Mary,
> bright dawn
> of the new world,
> Mother of the living,
> to you do we entrust
> the cause of life:
> Look down, O Mother,
> upon the vast numbers
> of babies not allowed
> to be born,
> of the poor whose lives
> are made difficult,
> of men and women who are
> victims of brutal violence,
> of the elderly
> and the sick killed
> by indifference
> or out of misguided mercy.
> Grant that all who
> believe in your Son may
> proclaim the Gospel of life
> with honesty and love
> to the people of our time.
> Obtain for them the grace
> to accept that Gospel
> as a gift ever new,
> the joy of celebrating it

> with gratitude throughout
> their lives and the courage
> to bear witness to it
> resolutely, in order
> to build, together with
> all people of good will,
> the civilization of
> truth and love,
> to the praise and glory
> of God, the Creator
> and lover of life.

- *Mercy Sunday, April 10, 1994*

John Paul II ends his *Regina Caeli* address with a prayer for trust to the Mother of Mercy:

O Mary, Mother of mercy! You know the heart of your divine Son better than anyone. Instill in us the filial trust in Jesus practiced by the saints, the trust that animated Blessed Faustina Kowalska, the great apostle of Divine Mercy in our time.

Look lovingly upon our misery: O Mother, draw us away from the contrary temptations of self-sufficiency and despair, and obtain for us an abundance of saving mercy.

- *Victory Strategy and Veritatis Splendor*

In his tenth encyclical, *Veritatis Splendor* (Splendor of the Truth) August 6, 1993, John Paul II revealed his "victory strategy" for overcoming the greatest moral problems of our times. In the conclusion of *Veritatis Splendor* he turns to the same "victory strategy" that he invoked in the defeat of Soviet atheistic communism.

It is commonly accepted that Pope John Paul II had a significant role in the dissolution of the U.S.S.R. It is even acknowledged by Mikhail Gorbachev and Time magazine. But the Holy Father attributes the victory not to himself, but to the Virgin

Mother of God.

The "victory strategy" of John Paul II is to entrust all to Mary, the Mother of God.

This was the victory strategy of the Primate of Poland, Stefan Cardinal Wyszynski who, while imprisoned by the communist Polish government, entrusted himself to Mary for the sake of the Church and the nation. He then arranged for a national renewal of vows to Mary on the 400th anniversary of the vows of King Kazimierz in thanksgiving to Mary for the victory over the Swedes at Jasna Gora. Over a million people gathered with the Polish bishops on May 3, 1956 at Jasna Gora to entrust the Church and the Polish nation to Mary. The next ten years were a novena in preparation for the solemn consecration of the nation marking the millennium of Christianity (May 3, 1966). Archbishop Karol Wojtyla preached the homily. Later when he returned to Poland as Pope he said:

> It seems to me that we have done something great, some-thing that first demands faith and that later will bring forth great fruit for the Holy Church in Poland and the world (June 4, 1979).

As the newly elected Pope, John Paul II dedicated his pon-tificate to Mary, using as his motto: *Totus Tuus*. On his first visit to Poland as Pope, he returned to Jasna Gora (June 4, 1979) and renewed the solemn vows to Mary:

> I entrust to you, Mother of the Church, all the workings of the Church, all its missions and all its service in perspec-tive of the second thousand years of Christianity that are now ending on earth.

Both the Primate and the Pope believed in the mediation of Mary for the freedom of the Church around the world and they wanted to entrust everything to her. Truly they believed that vic-tory in the universal Church, when it comes, will be her victo-ry (*Cardinal Wyszynski; a Biography*, Andrzej Micewski,

Harcourt Brace, 1984).

Pope John Paul II has continued this "victory strategy" in his pilgrimages around the world, entrusting each nation and the church at the various national shrines to Our Lady. His "victory strategy" reached a pinnacle of power as he knelt before the original Fatima statue of Mary on the square of St. Peter's Basilica on the Feast of the Annunciation, March 25, 1984, and entrusted all the nations of the world to the Mother of God, together with the bishops around the world. The bishops were asked to join in this collegial consecration in their local dioceses.

From that moment, a cascade of events started: Mikhail Gorbachev came into power and initiated *peristroika* and *glasnost*; solidarity came into power and one eastern European country after another shook off atheistic communism, beginning with Poland; the Berlin wall was torn down and the Soviet Union and communism in Eastern Europe dissolved.

John Paul II's "victory strategy" is entrustment to Mary – Give all to Mary, the woman of victory, in imitation of our heavenly Father who gave the promise of victory to the woman (Gen 3:15), and in imitation of Jesus, who gave all to His mother (Jn 19:26) in giving her His Church.

In his tenth and greatest encyclical, Veritatis Splendor, John Paul II applies his "victory strategy" to the great problems of our day – practical atheism and moral relativism. Practical atheism is a form of life without God and without truth. Moral relativism is a life separated from absolute truth – truth separated from God's laws, separated from laws of nature, separated from conscience and freedom – separated from the power of the Cross.

John Paul II concluded this encyclical by using his "victory strategy:" He entrusts all of mankind of good will and the research of moralists specifically to Mary, the Mother of God and Mother of Mercy:[3]

---

[3] For the full text of John Paul II's entrustment to the Mother of Mercy see Appendix.

At the end of these considerations, let us entrust ourselves, the sufferings and the joys of our life, the moral life of believers and people of good will, and the research of moralists, to Mary, Mother of God and Mother of Mercy (#118).

He then goes on to point out that Mary is Mother of Mercy because she is mother of her Son, Jesus, who revealed the mercy of the Father. He revealed the fullness of God's mercy by his passion, death, and resurrection, sending the Holy Spirit to give us new life and making it possible for us to do good and live the new life of "following Jesus Christ."

Mary is also Mother of Mercy because Jesus entrusted His Church and all of humanity to her. In her perfect docility to the Holy Spirit, she "obtains for us Divine Mercy."

Mary is the model of the moral life, John Paul II continues. "She lived and exercised her freedom precisely by giving herself to God ... and entered fully into the plan of God who gave Himself to the world." She truly is the "Seat of Wisdom."

Mary is compassionate and understands and loves sinful man as a mother. She is on the side of truth and shares the burden of the Church in calling all to the demands of morality and to the power of the Cross.

During his pilgrimage of thanksgiving to Fatima in 1982, John Paul II described consecration of the world to mercy as returning to the Cross of Christ. Later the next week at the Vatican *Regina Caeli* talk, he developed this theme of consecration as allowing Mary to bring us to the Cross of Jesus, to the source of all mercy:

Consecrating the world to the Immaculate Heart of the Mother means returning beneath the Cross of the Son. It means consecrating this world to the pierced Heart of the Savior, bringing it back to the very source of its Redemption. Redemption is always greater than man's sin and the "sin of the world." The power of the Redemption is infinitely superior to the whole range of evil in man and in the world (Homily, May 13, 1982).

In the conclusion of *Veritatis Splendor*, John Paul II writes of God's mercy:

No human sin can erase the mercy of God, or prevent Him from unleashing all His triumphant power, if we only call upon Him. Indeed, sin itself makes even more radiant the love of the Father who, in order to ransom a slave, sacrificed His Son.

Pope John Paul II, aware of the "victory strategy" of entrusting all to the Mother of Mercy prays in conclusion:

O Mary,
Mother of Mercy,
watch over all people,
that the Cross of Christ
may not be emptied of its power,
that man may not stray
from the path of the good
or become blind to sin,
but may put his hope ever more fully in God
Who is "rich in mercy" (Eph 2:4).
May he carry out the good works
prepared by God beforehand (cf Eph 2:10)
and so live completely
"for the praise of His glory" (Eph 1:12).

Chapter 12:   The Jubilee Year 2000

On the solemnity of the Assumption of Our Lady (Aug 15, 1999) John Paul II said in his homily that "the spirit of the Magnificat is the spirit of the Jubilee:"

"My soul magnifies the Lord!" (Lk 1:26). In this perspective, the Virgin of the *Magnificat* helps us to understand better the value and meaning of the Great Jubilee now at our door, a favorable time when the universal Church will join in her canticle to praise the wonder of the Incarnation.

The spirit of the *Magnificat* is the spirit of the Jubilee.

At John Paul II's election as Pope in 1978, Stephan Cardinal Wyszynski, the Primate of Poland told Pope John Paul II that "The Lord has called you [to be Pope]. You are to lead the Church into the third millennium." The Pope took this word as prophetic. In fact, so much so, that understanding the meaning of the Jubilee year as entering into the third millennium is key to understanding John Paul II's pontificate.

In his first encyclical, *Redeemer of Man*, he took up this task and then in *Tertio Millennio Adveniente*, November 10, 1994, (As the Third Millennium Draws Near) he laid out a plan of preparation for and celebration of the Jubilee Year 2000. The first phase (1995-1996) was to be a time of preparation, purification and prayer that introduced the second phase of three years. The year 1997 was devoted to Jesus Christ; the year 1998, to the Holy Spirit; and the year 1999, to the Father. The Jubilee Year of 2000 was to be celebrated in Rome and in churches throughout the world: a year that presented the goal and fulfillment of Christian life — intensely Eucharistic — with the theme of "Jesus Christ is the same, yesterday, today, and forever" (see Heb 13:8).

John Paul II gave a strong and clear challenge to the Church:

One thing is certain: Everyone is asked to do as much as possible to ensure that the great challenge of the Year 2000 is not overlooked, for this challenge certainly involves a special grace of the Lord for the Church and for the whole of humanity (T.M.A. #55).

In the official declaration of the Jubilee Year of 2000, Incarnationis Mysterium (*The Mystery of the Incarnation*), he called the Jubilee Year a "year of mercy" (#41) ; "an especially deep experience of mercy" (#6).

The celebration of the Jubilee Year for the Holy Father has been the summit of his life, with celebrations of mercy by forgiveness, pilgrimages to Egypt and Mount Sinai and then to the Holy Land. He called the celebration of Corpus Christi "the heart of the Jubilee Year".

Truly a high point of the Jubilee Year for the Holy Father, and a day of special joy, was the canonization of Saint Faustina:

Today my joy is truly great in presenting the life and witness of Sr. Faustina Kowalska to the whole Church as a gift of God for our time (Homily, April 30, 2000).... Sr. Faustina's canonization has a particular eloquence: by this act, I intend to pass this message on to the new millennium. I pass it on to all people, so that they will learn to know even better the true face of God and the true face of their brethren (#5, ibid).

The Jubilee Year is certainly a triumph of John Paul II's vision, planning and determination. Millions of pilgrims have swarmed to the heart of the Church for a deeper encounter with the Lord.

Chapter 13:   The Jubilee Year, The New Advent, The Third Millennium and the Coming of the Lord

The Jubilee Year of 2000 was the "year of mercy," the year of the door leading us into the new Advent and the opening up of the third millennium.

John Paul II writes of the "new Advent" in what can be called a mystical, or even prophetic sense. He wants and expects the Church to encounter the Lord in a new and deeper way. We need to allow the Holy Spirit to act as in a "new Pentecost."

A.   The Encyclicals that describe the Jubilee Year

John Paul II writes of a "new Advent" in each of the three encyclicals of the triad on the Holy Trinity in relationship to the new millennium:

• Redeemer of Man (*Redemptor Hominis*), his first encyclical, March 4, 1979:

We are in a certain way in a season of a new Advent, a season of expectation (#1).

What should we do, in order that this new Advent of the Church connected with the approaching end of the second millennium may bring us closer to Him whom Sacred Scripture calls "Everlasting Father" (Is. 9:6; RH #7)?

It is certain that the Church of the new Advent, the Church that is continually preparing for the new coming of the Lord, must be the Church of the Eucharist and of Penance (#20).

As I end this meditation with a warm and humble call to prayer, I wish the Church to devote herself to this prayer, together with Mary, the Mother of Jesus (see Acts 1:14), as the Apostles and disciples of the Lord did in the Upper Room in Jerusalem after His Ascension. Above all, I implore Mary, the heavenly Mother of the Church, to be so good as to devote herself to this prayer of humanity's new Advent, together with us who make up the Church, that is to say the Mystical Body of her Only Son. I hope that through this prayer we shall be able to receive the Holy Spirit coming upon us and thus be witnesses "to the end of the earth" (Acts 1:8), like those who went forth from the Upper Room in Jerusalem on the day of Pentecost (#22).

- *Rich in Mercy (Dives in Misericordia)* First Sunday of Advent, 1980:

The same mystery of Christ, which reveals to us the great vocation of man and which led me to emphasize in the Encyclical *Redemptor Hominis* his incomparable dignity, also obliges me to proclaim mercy as God's merciful love revealed in that same mystery of Christ. [This mystery of Christ] likewise obliges me to have recourse to that mercy and to beg for it at this difficult, critical phase of the history of the Church and of the world as we approach the end of the second millennium (#15).

- *Lord and Giver of Life (Dominum et Vivificantem)*, on the Holy Spirit in the life of the Church and World, Pentecost Sunday, 1986.

In the third encyclical of the trilogy on the Holy Trinity, John Paul II gives a thorough description of the Jubilee year and its transition to the third millennium. Eighteen times he refers to this transition.[4] A few highlights will illustrate the importance he placed on the Great Jubilee:

The great Jubilee will mark the passage from the second to the third Christian millennium (#2).

In Part II of the encyclical, John Paul II dedicates two sections to the "Reason for the Jubilee of the Year 2000":

1.   Christ, who was conceived of the Holy Spirit (#49).

---

[4] The eighteen references to the Jubilee Year and the transition to the millennium are given in the Appendix.

The Church cannot prepare for the Jubilee in another way than in the Holy Spirit (#51).

2. Grace has been made manifest (#52)

In the mystery of the Incarnation, the work of the Spirit "who gives life," reaches its highest point (#52).

The Pope ends his reflections on the Holy Spirit and the Great Jubilee by imploring the Holy Spirit for the peace and joy that are the fruit of love in the transition from the second to the third Christian millennium (#67).

B: The Message of Divine Mercy is the Message of the Third Millennium

On Mercy Sunday, April 30, 2000, in the homily for the canonization of St. Faustina, John Paul II stressed the message of Divine Mercy as the message for the third millennium:

Jesus told Sr. Faustina: "Mankind will not find peace until it turns with trust to My mercy" (Diary, #300). Through the work of [this] Polish religious, this message has been linked forever to the 20th century, the last of the second millennium and the bridge to the third .... the light of Divine Mercy, which the Lord in a way wished to return to the world through Sr. Faustina's charism, will illumine the way for men and women of the third millennium. ...

Sr. Faustina's canonization has a particular eloquence: by this act I intend today to pass this message on to the new millennium. I pass it on to all people (#2, 3, 5).

C: Two prophetic streams about the third millennium

In the March, 1999 issue of the *Renewal Ministries* newsletter, Ralph Martin described two prophetic streams about the future: John Paul II's prophetic announcement of a "new springtime" and Mary's urgent call to conversion.

The two streams may appear to be contradictory, but rather,

they are complementary. The scripture text that brings these two streams into a unity is Luke 7:31-35:

> "What comparison can I use for the men of today? What are they like? They are like children squatting in the city squares and calling to their playmates,
>
>> 'We piped you a tune but you did not dance,
>>
>> we sang you a dirge but you did not wail.'
>
> I mean that John the Baptist came neither eating bread nor drinking wine, and you say, 'He is mad!' The Son of Man came and he both ate and drank, and you say, 'Here is a glutton and a drunkard, a friend of tax collectors and sinners!' God's wisdom is vindicated by all who accept it."

Ralph Martin comments on the two different approaches of John Paul II and Mary:

> *Pope John Paul II* is piping a tune of "new springtime", of "new Pentecost", of a "Great Jubilee" – and there are many refusing to dance, to undergo the preparation "in the Holy Spirit" to become "docile to the Holy Spirit" which are preconditions for the coming of the new springtime.
>
> *Mary* is weeping, is singing a dirge, weeping for her children who are in danger of being swept away by the immense and proximate danger, the closeness of the chastisement and judgment, the danger of eternal death, of hell. And there are many who are refusing to have their hearts broken by her tears; there are many who are refusing to respond to the profound simplicity of her repeated calls to conversion. …
>
> John Paul is calling us to a dance of preparation for the "greatest Jubilee the Church has ever celebrated".
>
> Mary is weeping for those in danger of missing the visitation and has unveiled a personal plan of preparation for what is coming that involves prayer, fasting, repentance

and Reconciliation, daily Eucharist, rosary, conversion and faith.

These messages are complementary, they are two sides of one coin, two edges of one sword. It is urgent that we respond.

D: At the Beginning of the New Millennium

Novo Millennium Inuente, Apostolic Letter of Pope John Paul II, January 6, 2001, The Solemnity of the Epiphany.

In this letter, John Paul II reflects on and makes a general assessment of the Jubilee Year 2000, setting before the Church the challenge to "put out into the deep" (*Duc in Altum*, Lk 5:6) as we enter into the third millennium.

He gives thanks to the Lord for He is good, for His mercy endures forever (Ps 118:1) and he sings of the mercies of the Lord forever (Ps 89:2).

This Jubilee Year has been an experience of the three essential aspects [true hope, reconciliation, one unceasing hymn of praise of the Trinity], reaching moments of intensity which have made us as it were *touch with our hands the merciful presence of God...* (#4, emphasis added).

John Paul II challenges us "to contemplate the face of Christ" and "put out into the deep" (#15) – by a life of faith based on prayer and contemplation – allowing grace to take us by the hand. He calls us to the experience of silence and prayer which is the setting for development of faith (#20). Yes, he calls us to contemplate Christ's face of sorrow and of resurrection (#28). He calls us to "start afresh from Christ" (#29).

The Holy Father makes it clear that:

all pastoral initiations [in setting out into the deep] must be set in relationship to holiness (#30), prayer (#32), the Sunday Eucharist (#35), and the Sacrament of Reconciliation (#36).

In all of this planning we must observe the principle: "the primacy of grace" (#38). Throughout he calls us to mercy, to forgiveness, to compassion.

John Paul then reflects on the challenges of the third millennium: the need of the witness of love (#42), a spirituality of communion (#43), Ecumenism (#48), the works of charity and mercy (#49), as well as the challenges of the present: an ecological crisis, problems of peace, and fundamental human rights (#51).

He concludes with the challenge of *Duc in Altum!* Put out into the deep:

Let us go forward in hope! A New Millennium is opening before the Church like a vast ocean upon which we shall venture, relying on the help of Christ... (#58).

We need to initiate the zeal of St. Paul: "straining forward to what lies ahead, and press on towards the goal for the prize of the upward call in Christ Jesus" (Phil 3:13-14) (#58).

Appendix

Dives in Misericordia (from a new translation by Rev. George Kosicki, C.S.B. See above, Chapter Four), November, 1981

9. Mother of Mercy

These words of the Church at Easter: "I will sing of the mercies of the Lord forever," re-echo the full prophetic content of the words Mary uttered during her visit to Elizabeth, the wife of Zechariah: "His mercy is ... from generation to generation." At the very moment of the Incarnation, these words opened up a new perspective of salvation history. After the Resurrection of Christ, this perspective is new on both the historical and final (eschatological) level. From that time onwards, there is a succession of new generations of individuals in the immense human family, in ever-increasing size; there is also a succession of new generations of the People of God, marked with the sign of the Cross and of the Resurrection and "sealed" (cf 2 Cor 1:21-22) with the sign of the Paschal Mystery of Christ, the radical revelation of the mercy that Mary proclaimed on the threshold of her kinswoman's house: "His mercy is ... from generation to generation" (Lk 1:50).

Mary is also the one who experienced mercy in a remarkable and exceptional way, as no other person has. At the same time, still in an exceptional way, she paid for her share in revealing God's mercy by the sacrifice of her heart. This sacrifice is intimately linked with the Cross of her Son at the foot of which she was to stand on Calvary. Her sacrifice is a unique sharing in the revelation of mercy, that is, a sharing in the absolute fidelity of God to His own love, to the covenant that He willed from eternity and that He entered into in time with man, with the people, with humanity; it is a sharing in that revelation that was decisively fulfilled through the Cross. *No one has experienced to the same degree as the Mother of the Crucified One* the mystery of the Cross, the overwhelming encounter of divine transcendent justice with love: that "kiss" given by mercy to justice (cf Ps 85:11). No one as much as Mary has accepted into their heart that mystery, that truly divine dimension of the Redemption accomplished on Calvary by means of the death of her Son, together with the sacrifice of her maternal heart and with her final "fiat."

Mary, then, is also the one who knows to the fullest the mystery of God's mercy. She knows its price, she knows how great it is. In this sense we call her the *Mother of Mercy,* God's Mother (Theotokos) of Mercy or the Mother of the God of Mercy. Each one of these titles contains its own deep theological meaning. Each of them expresses the special preparation of her soul, of her whole personality, so that she was able to see through the complex events, first of Israel, then of every individual and the whole of humanity, that mercy "from generation to generation" (Lk 1:50) in which people share, according to the eternal design of the most Holy Trinity.

The above titles which we attribute to the God-bearer speak of her above all, however, as the Mother of the Crucified and Risen One; as *the one* who experienced mercy *in an exceptional way,* and in an equally exceptional way "merits" that mercy throughout her earthly life and particularly at the foot of the Cross of her Son. Finally, these titles speak of her as the one who, through her hidden and at the same time incomparable sharing in the messianic mission of her Son, was called in a special way to bring close to people that love which He had come to reveal. That love finds its most concrete expression in all of the suffering, the poor, those deprived of their own freedom, the blind, the oppressed and sinners; just as Christ spoke of Isaiah, first in the synagogue at Nazareth (cf Lk 4:18) and then in response to the question of the messengers of John the Baptist (cf Lk 7:22).

Mary shared precisely in this "Merciful" love, which proves itself above all in contact with moral and physical evil. She shared singularly and exceptionally by her heart as the Mother of the Crucified and Risen One. This "merciful" love does not cease to be revealed in her and through her in the history of the Church and all mankind. This revelation is especially fruitful, because it is based on the remarkable docility of the maternal heart of the God-bearer, on her unique sensitivity and fitness to reach all who accept this merciful love most easily from a mother's side. This is one of the great life-giving mysteries of Christianity, a mystery intimately connected with the mystery of the Incarnation.

"The motherhood of Mary in the order of grace," as the Second Vatican Council explains, "lasts without interruption from the consent she faithfully gave at the Annunciation and which she sustained without hesitation under the Cross, until the eternal fulfillment of all the elect. In fact, being assumed into heaven she has not laid aside this office of salvation, but by her manifold intercession she continues to obtain for us graces of eternal salvation. By her maternal charity, she takes care of the brethren of her Son who still journey on earth, surrounded by dangers and difficulties, until they are led into their blessed home" (*Lumen Gentium*, #62).

The Jubilee Year Announcement in Lord and Giver of Life *(Dominum et Vivificantem)* – on the Holy Spirit in the Life of the Church and World, Pentecost Sunday, 1986

John Paul II gives a thorough description of the role of the Jubilee Year of 2000:

- The Church feels herself called to this mission of proclaiming the Spirit, while together with the human family she approaches *the end of the second Millennium after Christ* (# 2).

- The great Jubilee will mark the passage from the second to the third Christian Millennium (# 2).

- In our own century, when humanity is already close to the

end of the second Millennium after Christ, this era of the Church expressed itself in a special way through the Second Vatican Council. As the Council of our century. ... We can say that in its rich variety of teaching the Second Vatican Council contains precisely all that "the Spirit says to the Churches" (Rev. 2:29; 3:6,13, 22) with regard to the present phase of the history of salvation (# 26).

In Part III of the Encyclical "The Spirit who Gives Life," John Paul II gives the first "Reason for the Jubilee of the year 2000: Christ who was conceived of the Holy Spirit:"

- The *Church's mind and heart* turn to *the Holy Spirit as this twentieth century draws to a close* and the *third Millennium* since the coming of Jesus Christ into the world *approaches,* and as we look towards the *great Jubilee* with which the Church will celebrate the event (# 49).

- The *great Jubilee* at the close of the second Millennium, for which the Church is already preparing, has a directly *Christological aspect:* for it is a celebration of the birth of Jesus Christ. At the same time it has a *pneumatological aspect,* since the mystery of the Incarnation was accomplished "by the power of the Holy Spirit" (# 50).

- The conception and birth of Jesus Christ are in fact the greatest work accomplished by the Holy Spirit in the history of creation and salvation: the supreme grace – "the grace of union," source of every other grace, as St. Thomas explains (cf St. Thomas Aquinas, Summa Theologica IIIa, q.2, aa. 10-12; q.6, a.6; q.7, a. 13) *The great Jubilee* refers to this work and also – if we penetrate its depths – to the author of this work, *to the person of the Holy Spirit* (# 50).

- All this is accomplished by the power of the Holy Spirit, and so is part of the great Jubilee. The Church cannot prepare for the Jubilee in any other way than *in the Holy Spirit* (# 51).

John Paul II develops a second "Reason for the Jubilee: *grace has been made manifest:*

- In the mystery of the Incarnation the *work of the Spirit "who gives life"* reaches its highest point (#52).

All the graces of creation, adoption as children of God, our redemption and sanctification:

- *All this* may be said to fall within the scope of the great Jubilee (# 53).

- The great Jubilee to be celebrated at the end of this Millennium and at the beginning of the next ought to constitute a powerful call to all those who "worship God in Spirit and truth" (# 54).

- The Church's entire life, as will appear in the great Jubilee, means going to meet the invisible God, the hidden God: a meeting with the Spirit "who gives life" (# 54).

John Paul II states a prophetic sense about the new Advent and the Third Millennium:

- Against this background [of anti-religious materialism] so characteristic of our time, in preparing for the great Jubilee we must emphasize the "desires of the Spirit," as exhortations echoing in the night of a new time of Advent, at the end of which, like two thousand years ago, "every man will see the salvation of God" (Lk 3:6; cf. Is 40:5) (# 56).

The Jubilee calls for a gift of self:

- *As the year 2000* since the birth of Christ *draws near,* it is a question of ensuring that an ever greater number of people "may fully find themselves ... through a sincere gift of self" (#59).

- The great Jubilee of the year 2000 thus contains a message of liberation by the power of the Spirit (# 60).

As the end of the second Millennium approaches, we recall the coming of the Lord:

- The most complete sacramental expression of the "departure" of Christ through the Mystery of the Cross and Resurrection is the *Eucharist.* In every celebration of the Eucharist his coming, his salvific presence, is sacramentally realized: in the Sacrifice and in Communion (# 62).

- In the time leading up to the third Millennium after Christ, while "the Spirit and the bride say to the Lord Jesus: Come!," this prayer of theirs is filled, as always, with an eschatological significance, which is also destined to give fullness of meaning to the celebration of the great Jubilee (#66).

- The Church wishes *to prepare* for this Jubilee *in the Holy Spirit,* just as the Virgin of Nazareth in whom the Word was made flesh was prepared by the Holy Spirit. (# 66).

The Easter message of the merciful Christ, General Audience, April 10, 1991

(*L'Osservatore Romano,* April 15, 1991)

This is the 53rd talk in the "Jasna Gora Cycle," a series of meditations which the Holy Father is using to prepare for his forthcoming trip to Poland. He gave it at the General Audience 10 April, 1991.

1.   In the name of Jesus Christ crucified and risen, in the spirit of His messianic mission, enduring in the history of humanity, we raise our voices and pray that the love which is in the Father may once again *be revealed at this stage of history* and that, through the work of the Son and Holy Spirit, it may be shown to be present in our modern world and to be more powerful than evil: more powerful than sin and death.

We pray for this through the intercession of her who does not cease to proclaim 'mercy... from generation to generation', and also through the intercession of those for whom there have been completely fulfilled the words of the Sermon on the Mount: 'Blessed are the merciful, for they shall obtain mercy'" (Mt 5:7) (*Dives in Misericordia*, #15).

2.   Our Lady of Jasna Gora! *The words of the encyclical on Divine Mercy (Dives in Misericordia)* are particularly close to us. They recall the figure of the Servant of God, Sister Faustina Kowalska. This simple woman religious particularly brought *the Easter message of the merciful Christ* closer to Poland and the whole world.

This happened before the Second World War and all its cruelty. In the face of all the organized contempt for the human person, the message of Christ who was tormented and rose again became for many people in Poland and beyond its borders, and even on other continents, *a source of the hope and strength necessary for survival.*

3.   And today? Is it perhaps not necessary also "in the contemporary world" in our homeland, in society, among the people who have entered into a new phase of our history, *for love to reveal that it is stronger than hatred and selfishness?* Is it perhaps not necessary to translate into the language of today's generations the words of the Gospel, "blessed are the merciful, for they shall obtain mercy" (Mt 5:7)?

O Mother, who announces Divine Mercy "from generation to generation" (Lk 1:50), help our generation *to rise from the moral crisis.* May Christ's new commandment, "love one another" (Jn 13:34) be established ever more fully among us.

Re: "The Easter Message of the Merciful Christ"

Significant points in regard to St. Faustina and the message of Divine Mercy:

- That St. Faustina is mentioned in print in the *L'Osservatore Romano* – a breakthrough.

- That St. Faustina is related to the encyclical, *Dives in Misericordia.*

- That St. Faustina illustrates the need for mercy – before World War II and *now*!

- The message is called the "*Easter* message of the merciful Christ" – it ties in with the Feast being part of the Easter message.

- A preparation for John Paul II's visit to Poland where he will bless the new Shrine at Plock where St. Faustina had the vision of the "Image" (February 22, 1931).

Homily, Divine Mercy Sunday, April 18, 1993

(L'Osservatore Romano, April 21, 1993)

On Sunday, April 18, Sister Faustina was beatified by Pope John Paul II in St. Peter's Square in Vatican City during a Mass celebrated with over 100,000 pilgrims from all over the world. During the Mass the Pope preached the homily in Italian, Spanish, Polish, and English, based on the readings for the Second Sunday of Easter. The following excerpts are taken from that homily.

"Give thanks to the Lord for He is good, for His mercy endures forever" (Ps 118 [117]: 1).

Like a band of light this psalm of thanksgiving passes through the Octave of Easter. It is the choral "thank you" of the Church which adores God for the gift of Christ's resurrection: for the gift of new and eternal life revealed in the risen Lord. With one heart the Church adores and thanks Him for the infinite love which has been communicated to every person and to the whole universe in Him. ...

I salute you, Sister Faustina. Beginning today the Church calls you Blessed, especially the Church in Poland and Lithuania. O Faustina, how extraordinary your life is! Precisely you, the poor and simple daughter of Mazovia, of the Polish people, were chosen by Christ to remind people of this great mystery of Divine Mercy! You bore this mystery within yourself, leaving this world after a short life, filled with suffering. However, at the same time, this mystery has become a prophetic reminder to the world, to Europe. Your message of Divine Mercy was born almost on the eve of World War II. Certainly you would have been amazed if you could have experienced upon this earth what this message meant for the suffering people during that hour of torment, and how it spread throughout the world. Today, we truly believe, you contemplate in God the fruits of your mission on earth. Today you experience it at its very source, which is your Christ, "dives in misericordia."

"I clearly feel that my mission does not end with death, but begins," Sister Faustina wrote in her diary. And it truly did! Her mission continues and is yielding astonishing fruit. It is truly marvelous how her devotion to the merciful Jesus is spreading in our contemporary world and gaining so many human hearts! This is doubtlessly *a sign of the times – a sign of our 20th century.* The balance of this century which is now ending, in addition to the advances which have often surpassed those of preceding eras, presents a deep restlessness and fear of the future. Where, if not in The Divine Mercy, can the world find refuge and the light of hope? Believers understand that perfectly.

"Give thanks to the Lord, for He is good. Give thanks to the Lord, for He is merciful."

Today, on the day of the Beatification of Sister Faustina, we praise the Lord for the great things He has done in her soul, we praise and thank Him for the great things He has done and always continues to do in the souls who through Sister Faustina's witness and message discover the infinite depths of The Divine Mercy.

General Audience, April 19, 1993

(L'Osservatore Romano, Monday-Tuesday, April 19-20, 1993)

"The example of the newly Beatified accompany you on your daily Christian walk." This is the wish expressed by John Paul II to the thousands of pilgrims gathered in Rome to participate in the solemn rite of beatification of Sunday, the 18th, and received in audience on the morning of Monday, the 19th. During the meeting, that took place in St. Peter's Square, the Pope pronounced the following discourse:

1.   I greet all of you, dearest brothers and sisters, who have come to Rome to render homage to the newly beatified.

Our encounter today represents a joyous prolongation of the solemn celebration that took place yesterday in this very square. With you I praise the Lord for such an extraordinary spiritual experience, and I wish everyone to give faithful witness to the Gospel, imitating the luminous examples of these servants of God, elevated to the honors of the altar. [...]

2.   Words of greeting I direct, next, to the Sisters of the Congregation of Our Lady of Mercy and to the numerous devotees of The Divine Mercy, gathered in Rome from many regions of Italy for the Beatification of Sister Faustina Kowalska. Yesterday has been a great day for all of you.

Dearly beloved, be apostles, by your word and your works, of the divine merciful love revealed to the highest degree in Jesus Christ. We are speaking of a mystery that, in a certain sense, is for all people the fountain of a life different from that which human beings are in a position to build with their own strength (cf Dives in Misericordia, #14).

May this mystery be for every one of you the inspiration and the strength to carry out the Divine Mercy in actual life. In the name of this mystery, Christ teaches us to pardon always and to love one another reciprocally as he himself has loved us.

"God rich in mercy"(cf Eph 2:4) bless you and make fruitful

your apostolic commitment.

6. Since we came back to Sr. Faustina, one more wish, that these simple words "Jesus, I trust in You!" that I see here on so many images, continually be for human hearts also in the future, near the end of this century and this millennium, and the next, a clear indicator of the way. "Jesus I trust in You." There is no such darkness in which man would need to lose himself. If only he will put his trust in Jesus, he will always find himself in the light. Praised be Jesus Christ!

Veritatis Splendor, August, 1993

CONCLUSION

Mary, Mother of Mercy

118. At the end of these considerations, let us entrust our-selves, the sufferings and the joys of our life, the moral life of believers and people of good will, and the research of moralists, to Mary, Mother of God and Mother of Mercy.

Mary is Mother of Mercy because her Son, Jesus Christ, was sent by the Father as the revelation of God's mercy (cf Jn 3:16-18). Christ came not to condemn but to forgive, to show mercy (cf Mt 9:13). And the greatest mercy of all is found in His being in our midst and calling us to meet Him and to con-fess, with Peter, that He is "the Son of the living God" (Mt 16:16). No human sin can erase the mercy of God, or prevent Him from unleashing all His triumphant power, if we only call upon Him. Indeed, sin itself makes even more radiant the love of the Father who, in order to ransom a slave, sacrificed His Son: His mercy towards us is Redemption. This mercy reaches its fullness in the gift of the Spirit who bestows new life and demands that it be lived. No matter how many and great the obstacles put in His way by human frailty and sin, the Spirit, who renews the face of the earth (cf Ps 104:30), makes possi-ble the miracle of the perfect accomplishment of the good. This renewal, which gives the ability to do what is good, noble, beautiful, pleasing to God and in conformity with His will, is in some way the flowering of the gift of mercy, which offers liberation from the slavery of evil and gives the strength to sin no more. Through the gift of new life, Jesus makes us sharers in His love and leads us to the Father in the Spirit.

119. Such is the consoling certainty of Christian faith, the source of its profound humanity and extraordinary simplicity. At times, in the discussions about new and complex moral problems, it can seem that Christian morality is in itself too demanding, difficult to understand and almost impossible to practice. This is untrue, since Christian morality consists, in the simplicity of the Gospel, in *following Jesus Christ*, in abandoning oneself to Him, in letting oneself be transformed by His grace and renewed by His mercy, gifts which come to us in the living communion of His Church. Saint Augustine reminds us that "he who would live has a place to live, and has everything needed to live. Let him draw near, let him believe, let him become part of the body, that he may have life. Let him not shrink from the unity of the members" (In Iohannis Evangelium Tractatus, 26, 13: CCL, 36, 266). By the light of the Holy Spirit, the living essence of Christian morality can be understood by everyone, even the least learned, but particularly those who are able to preserve an "undivided heart" (Ps 86:11). On the other hand, this evangelical simplicity does not exempt one from facing reality in its complexity; rather it can lead to a more genuine understanding of reality, inasmuch as following Christ will gradually bring out the distinctive character of authentic Christian morality, while providing the vital energy needed to carry it out. It is the task of the Church's Magisterium to see that the dynamic process of following Christ develops in an organic manner, without the falsification or obscuring of its moral demands, with all their consequences. The one who loves Christ keeps His commandments (cf Jn 14:15).

120. Mary is also Mother of Mercy because it is to her that

Jesus entrusts his Church and all humanity. At the foot of the Cross, when she accepts John as her son, when she asks, together with Christ, forgiveness from the Father for those who do not know what they do (cf Lk 23:34), Mary experiences, in perfect docility to the Spirit, the richness and the universality of God's love, which opens her heart and enables it to embrace the entire human race. Thus Mary becomes Mother of each and every one of us, the Mother who obtains for us Divine Mercy.

Mary is the radiant sign and inviting model of the moral life. As Saint Ambrose put it, "The life of this one person can serve as a model for everyone" (de Virginibus, Bk. II, Chap .II, 15: PL 16, 222), and while speaking specifically to virgins but within a context open to all, he affirmed: "The first stimulus to learning is the nobility of the teacher. Who can be more noble than the Mother of God? Who can be more glorious than the one chosen by Glory Itself?" (De Virginibus, Bk. II, Chap. II, 7: PL 16, 220.) Mary lived and exercised her freedom precisely by giving herself to God and accepting God's gift within herself. Until the time of his birth, she sheltered in her womb the Son of God who became man; she raised Him and enabled Him to grow, and she accompanied Him in that supreme act of freedom which is the complete sacrifice of His own life. By the gift of herself, Mary entered fully into the plan of God who gives Himself to the world. By accepting and pondering in her heart events which she did not always understand (cf. Lk 2:19), she became the model of all those who hear the word of God and keep it (cf Lk 11:28), and merited the title of "Seat of Wisdom". This Wisdom is Jesus Christ Himself, the Eternal Word of God, who perfectly reveals and accomplishes the will of the Father (cf Heb 10:5-10). Mary invites everyone to accept this Wisdom. To us too, she addresses the command she gave to the servants at Cana in Galilee during the marriage feast: "Do whatever he tells you" (Jn 2:5).

Mary shares our human condition, but in complete openness to the grace of God. Not having known sin, she is able to have compassion on every kind of weakness. She understands sinful man and loves him with a Mother's love. Precisely for this reason she is on the side of truth and shares the Church's burden in recalling always and to everyone the demands of morality. Nor does she permit sinful man to be deceived by those who claim to love him by justifying his sin, for she knows that the sacrifice of Christ her Son would thus be emptied of its power. No absolution offered by beguiling doctrines, even in the areas of philosophy and theology, can make man truly happy: only the Cross and the glory of the Risen Christ can grant peace to his conscience and salvation to his life.

> O Mary,
> Mother of Mercy,
> watch over all people,
> that the Cross of Christ
> may not be emptied of its power,
> that man may not stray
> from the path of the good
> or become blind to sin,
> but may put his hope ever more fully in God
> who is "rich in mercy" (Eph 2:4).
> May he carry out the good works prepared
> by God beforehand (cf Eph 2:10)
> and so live completely
> "for the praise of his glory" (Eph 1:12).

Given in Rome, at Saint Peter's, on 6 August, Feast of the Transfiguration of the Lord, in the year 1993, the fifteenth of my Pontificate.

Regina Caeli, Divine Mercy Sunday, April 10, 1994:
Christ's peace is the triumph of Divine Mercy

(L'Osservatore Romano, April 13, 1994)

On Sunday April 10, before praying the Regina Caeli, the Holy Father reflected on the peace Christ brought by his resurrection and the triumph of Divine Mercy.

1. *"Peace be with you!"*. This is the greeting of the risen Christ, which has been echoed several times in our biblical readings during this Octave of Easter and in particular, in the Gospel of today's liturgy. On Jesus' lips this greeting goes far beyond the perspective of and desire for external peace, although this is so necessary. The peace brought by Jesus is the *fullness of the Easter gift.*

Christ Himself is *our peace* (cf Eph 2:14). Appearing to the Apostles after the resurrection, He, the Lamb of God who takes away the sin of the world (cf Jn 1:29), inaugurates *the time of great mercy offered to mankind through the gift of the Spirit and the sacraments of the Church: "Whose sins you forgive are forgiven them"* (Jn 20:23).

2. The peace brought by the Risen One is consequently the *triumph of Divine Mercy.* What is mercy if not the boundless love of God, who, confronted with human sin, restrains the sentiment of severe justice and, allowing himself to be moved by the wretchedness of His creatures, spurs Himself to the total gift of self, in the Son's cross? "O happy fault ... which gained for us so great a Redeemer!" (Easter Proclamation).

To understand the depth of this mystery, we should take Jesus' disconcerting revelation seriously: "... there will be more joy in heaven over one sinner who repents than over ninety-nine righteous people who have no need of repentance" (Lk 15:7). God is truly the Shepherd who leaves ninety-nine sheep to go in search of the one that has strayed (cf Lk 15:4-6); he is the Father who is always ready to welcome a lost son (cf Lk 15:11-

31). Who can say he is free from sin and does not need God's mercy?

As people of this restless time of ours, wavering between the emptiness of self-exaltation and the humiliation of despair, we have a greater need than ever for a regenerating experience of mercy. We should learn to say repeatedly to God with the faith and simplicity of children: "Great is our sin, but even greater is your love!" (Vespers hymn during the season of Lent).

Opening ourselves to mercy, we must not be content with mediocrity and sin, but on the contrary, we must be revived by resolutions to lead a new life.

3.   O Mary, Mother of Mercy! You know the heart of your divine Son better than anyone. Instill in us the filial trust in Jesus practiced by the saints, the trust that animated Blessed Faustina Kowalska, the great apostle of Divine Mercy in our time.

Look lovingly upon our misery: O Mother, draw us away from the contrary temptations of self-sufficiency and despair, and obtain for us an abundance of saving mercy.

CONGREGATIO DE CULTU DIVINO ET DISCIPLINA SACRAMENTORUM
Prot. 822/93/L

FOR POLAND

In recent times, the clergy and faithful of Poland, have come to a deeper understanding of – and hence devotion to – "The Mercy of God," that is, "The Merciful Jesus." This has been evidenced by a greatly renewed sacramental life, as well as by widespread and greatly increased works of charity.

Indeed, this specific type of devotion leads by its very nature to the Lord and God who is to be glorified as "rich in mercy," above all in the celebration of the Paschal Mystery, in which the Mercy of God for all men shines forth most brilliantly.

In view of these facts, and also taking into consideration the request made by their Eminences the Cardinals, and their Excellencies the Archbishops and Bishops of Poland, set out in their letter of March 23, 1993, the Supreme Pontiff JOHN PAUL II graciously grants that, hereafter in the dioceses of Poland, to the title, "The Second Sunday of Easter," there be added this specification, "namely, Divine Mercy Sunday," prescribing also that, in the liturgical celebration of the aforementioned Sunday, the texts for that day found in the Roman Missal and in the Liturgy of the Hours be always adhered to.

We are communicating these directives of the Supreme Pontiff to the concerned parties, in order that they be duly carried out.

Anything whatsoever to the contrary notwithstanding.

Given at the Office of the Congregation for Divine Worship and the Discipline of the Sacraments, on this 23rd day of January, 1995.

(Antonius M. Card. Javierre)
Prefect

(+ Gerardus M. Agnelo)
Archbishop Secretary

(Unofficial translation from the original Latin document by Archbishop George Pearce, S.M.)

Homily at the Church of the Holy Spirit, Divine Mercy Sunday, April 23, 1995:

Be Apostles of Divine Mercy

(L'Osservatore Romano, May 3, 1995)

"The mystical experience of Blessed Faustina Kowalska and her cry to the merciful Christ belong to the harsh context of our century's history," the Holy Father said on the Sunday of Divine Mercy, 23 April, as he celebrated Mass in the Roman Church of the Holy Spirit "in Sassia."

1.   *"Peace be with you!"* (Jn 20:19).

The Risen Jesus said these words twice on appearing to the Eleven in the Upper Room, on the evening of the very day when He rose from the dead. The Lord, as the Evangelist John testifies, showed them His hands and His side, to *confirm* in their presence *the identity of His body*, as if to say: this is the same body that two days ago was nailed to the cross and then laid in the tomb; the body that bears the wounds of the crucifixion and the stab of the lance. It is the direct proof that I have risen and am alive.

From the human point of view, this observation was difficult to accept as *Thomas' reaction shows.* On the evening of the first appearance in the Upper Room, Thomas was absent. And when the other Apostles told him they had seen the Lord, *he firmly refused to believe them:* "Unless I see the mark of the nails in His hands and put my finger into the nail marks and put my hand into His side, I will not believe" (Jn 20:25). From these words it can be seen *how important Christ's physical identity was for the truth of the Resurrection.*

When the Lord Jesus, on the eighth day – like today – again entered the Upper Room, He addressed Thomas directly, as if to satisfy his request: "Put your finger here and see My hands, and bring your hand and put it into My side, and do not be unbelieving, but believe" (Jn 20:27). Faced with such proof, the

Apostle not only believed but drew the ultimate conclusion of what he had seen and expressed it in the highest and briefest profession of faith: "My Lord and my God!" (Jn 20:28). *In the presence of the Risen One, the truth both of His humanity and of His divinity became clear to Thomas.* The One who had risen by His own power was the Lord: "The Lord of life does not know death" (from a Polish Easter hymn).

Thomas' confession ends the series of witnesses to Christ's Resurrection which the Church presents during the Octave of Easter. *"My Lord and my God!"*. Replying to these words, *Jesus, in a certain sense, discloses the reality of His Resurrection to the future of all human history.* In fact, He says to Thomas: "Have you come to believe because you have seen Me? *Blessed are those who have not seen and have believed"* (Jn 20:29). He was thinking of those who would not see Him risen, nor eat and drink with Him as the Apostles had (cf Acts 10:41), and yet would believe on the basis of eye-witnesses' accounts. They are the ones, in particular, to be called "blessed" by Christ.

I live forever that man may share in immortal life

2.   *"Do not be afraid. I am the First and the Last, the One who lives"* (Rv 1:17).

There is a certain analogy between the appearance in the Upper Room – especially that of the eighth day, in Thomas' presence – and the eschatological vision St. John speaks of in the second reading from Revelation. In the Upper Room Christ shows the Apostles, and especially Thomas, the wounds in His hands, His feet and His side, to confirm the identity of His risen and glorious body with the one that was crucified and laid in the tomb. In Revelation, the Lord introduced Himself as the First and the Last, as the One from whom the history of the cosmos begins and with whom it ends, the One who is "the firstborn of all creation" (Col 1:15), "the firstborn from the dead" (Col 1:18), the beginning and the end of human history.

His identity, *which endlessly pervades the history of men*, is formulated with the words: "Once I was dead, but now I am alive for ever and ever" (Rv 1:18). It is as if He had said: in time I was dead; I accepted death to remain faithful to the very end to the Incarnation through which, remaining the Son of God consubstantial with the Father, I became true man in everything except sin (cf Heb 4:15). The three days of My Passion and Death, necessary for the work of Redemption, remain in Me and in you. And now I live forever and, with my Resurrection, show forth the will of God who calls every man to share in My own immortal life. I have the keys of death with which I must open earthly tombs and change cemeteries from places where death reigns into vast spaces for the resurrection.

3. "Do not be afraid!". When, on the island of Patmos, Jesus addresses this exhortation to John, He reveals his victory over the many fears that accompany man in his earthly existence and especially *when he is faced with suffering and death*. The fear of death also concerns the *great unknown which it represents*. Could it be a total annihilation of the human being? Do not the severe words: *"For you are dust, and to dust you shall return"* (cf Gn 3:19) fully express the harsh reality of death? Thus man has serious reasons to feel afraid when he faces the mystery of death.

Contemporary civilization does all it can to *distract human attention from the inescapable reality of death* and tries to induce man *to live as though death did not exist*. And this is expressed practically in the attempt to *turn man's conscience away from God:* to make him live as through God did not exist! But the reality of death is obvious. It is impossible to silence it; it is impossible to dispel the fear associated with it.

Man fears death as he fears what comes after death. *He fears judgment and punishment, and this fear has a saving value:* it should not be eliminated in man. When Christ says: "Do not be afraid!", He wants to respond to *the deepest source of the human being's existential fear.* What He means is: Do not fear evil, since in My Resurrection good has shown itself stronger than evil. My Gospel is victorious truth. Life and death met on Calvary in a stupendous combat and life proved victorious: *"Dux vitae mortuus regnat vivus!"*, "Once I was dead, but now I am alive for ever and ever" (Rv 1:18).

4.   "The stone which the builders rejected has become the cornerstone" (Ps 117 [118]: 22). The verse of the responsorial psalm in today's liturgy helps us to understand the truth about Christ's Resurrection. *It also expresses the truth about Divine Mercy, revealed in the Resurrection: love gained the victory over sin, and life over death.* In a certain sense, this truth is the very essence of the Good News. Therefore Christ can say: Do not be afraid!". He repeats these words to every man, especially to those who are suffering physically or spiritually. He can justifiably repeat them.

Sr. Faustina Kowalska heralded God's mercy

Sr. Faustina Kowalska, whom I had the joy of beatifying two years ago, especially understood this. Her mystical experiences were all focused on the *mystery of the merciful Christ* and are a remarkable commentary as it were on the word of God presented to us in this Sunday's liturgy. Sr. Faustina not only recorded them, but sought an artist who could paint the image of the merciful Christ just as she saw Him. An image which, together with the figure of Blessed Faustina, is an eloquent testimony to what theologians call *"condescendentia divina".* God makes Himself understandable to His human interlocutors. Sacred Scripture, and especially the Gospel, confirm this..

Dear brothers and sisters, Sr. Faustina's message follows these lines. But was it only Sr. Faustina's, or rather, *was it not at the same time a testimony given by all those who were encouraged by this message in the cruel experiences of the Second World War, in the concentration and extermination camps, and in the bombings?* The mystical experience of

Blessed Faustina Kowalska and her cry to the merciful Christ belong to the harsh context of our century's history. As people of this century which is now coming to an end, *we would like to thank the Lord for the message of Divine Mercy.*

5.   Today in particular, I am pleased to be able to give thanks to God in this *Church of the Holy Spirit "in Sassia"* attached to the hospital of the same name and now a *specialized center for the pastoral care of the sick as well as for the promotion of the spirituality of Divine Mercy.* It is very significant and timely that precisely here, next to this very ancient hospital, prayers are said and work is done with constant care for the health of body and spirit. As I express again my satisfaction to the Cardinal Vicar, I also address a grateful thought to the titular, Cardinal Fiorenzo Angelini. I greet the Bishop of the western sector, the rector and the other priests, the sisters and all of you, dear faithful, who are present here. I would also like to convey fraternal wishes to the patients of Santo Spirito Hospital, as well as to the doctors, nurses, sisters and all those who help them every day. I would like to say to all: trust in the Lord! Be apostles of Divine Mercy and, following the invitation and the example of Blessed Faustina, take care of those who suffer in body and especially in spirit. Let each one feel the merciful love of the Lord who comforts and instills joy.

May Jesus be your peace!

"Jesus Christ is the same yesterday, today and forever!" (Heb 13:8)

Contemplating Him in the mystery of the Cross and the Resurrection, let us repeat together with this Sunday's liturgy:

"Give thanks to the Lord, for He is good, for His mercy endures forever!"

Regina Caeli Address, Divine Mercy Sunday, April 23, 1995:

New Life and Joy flow from Easter

L'Osservatore Romano, April 26, 1995

"The spiral of hatred and violence which stains with blood the path of so many individuals and nations can only be broken by the miracle of forgiveness", the Holy Father said to the crowds gathered in St. Peter's Square on Sunday, 23 April, before praying the Regina Caeli.

Dear Brothers and Sisters,

1.   Today ends the Octave of Easter, when the Church repeats the words of the Psalm with exultation: "This is the day the Lord has made; let us be glad and rejoice in it" (Ps 117 [118]: 24). *The whole Octave is like a single day, the new day, the day of the new creation.* By conquering death, Christ has made all things new (cf Rv 21:5). From Easter flows *new life, new peace and new joy* for all believers.

However, the peace and joy of Easter are not only for the Church: they are for the whole world! Joy is victory over fear, violence and death. Peace is the antithesis of anguish. Greeting the Apostles, who were frightened and discouraged by His passion and death, the Risen One says: "Peace be with you" (Jn 20:19). When Christ appeared to John on the island of Patmos, this was once again His invitation: "Do not be afraid. I am the First and the Last, the One who lives. Once I was dead, but now I am alive for ever and ever. I hold the keys to death and the nether world" (Rv 1:17-18).

Easter overcomes human fear because it gives the only true answer to one of man's greatest problems: death. In proclaiming Jesus' Resurrection, the Church wishes to pass on to humanity *faith in the resurrection of the dead* and in everlasting life. The Christian proclamation is essentially "the Gospel of life".

2.   *Give thanks to the Lord, for he is good* (cf Psalm 117 [118]:1). In a special way, today is the Sunday of thanksgiving for the goodness God has shown man in the whole Easter mystery. This is why it is also called *the Sunday of Divine Mercy*. Essentially, God's mercy, as the mystical experience of Blessed Faustina Kowalska, who was raised to the honors of the altar two years ago, helps us to understand, reveals precisely this truth: good triumphs over evil, life is stronger than death and God's love is more powerful than sin. All this is manifested in Christ's Paschal Mystery, in which God appears to us as He is: a tender-hearted *Father*, who does not give up in the face of His children's ingratitude and is always ready to forgive.

3.   Dear brothers and sisters, we must personally experience this mercy if, in turn, we want to be capable of mercy. *Let us learn to forgive!* The spiral of hatred and violence which stains with blood the path of so many individuals and nations can only be broken by the *miracle of forgiveness.*

May Mary obtain this gift of Divine Mercy for all humanity so that the individuals and peoples who are particularly tormented by hostility and fratricidal war may overcome hatred and build concrete attitudes of reconciliation and peace.

Shrine of Divine Mercy in Poland, June 7, 1997

"Misericordias Domini in aeternum cantabo" ["I will sing the mercies of the Lord forever" – Ps 89:2].

I have come here to this shrine as a pilgrim to take part in the unending hymn in honor of Divine Mercy. The psalmist of the Lord had intoned it, expressing what every generation preserved and will continue to preserve as a most precious fruit of faith.

There is nothing that man needs more than Divine Mercy – that love which is benevolent, which is compassionate, which raises man above his weakness to the infinite heights of the holiness of God.

In this place we become particularly aware of this. From here, in fact, went out the Message of Divine Mercy that Christ himself chose to pass on to our generation through Blessed Faustina.

And it is a *message that is clear and understandable for everyone.* Anyone can come here, look at this image of the merciful Jesus, His Heart radiating grace, and hear in the depths of his own soul what Blessed Faustina heard: *"Fear nothing; I am always with you"* (Diary, 586).

And if this person responds with a sincere heart: *"Jesus, I trust in you,"* he will find comfort in all his *anxieties and fears.* In this "dialogue of abandonment," there is established between man and Christ a *special bond that sets love free.* And "there is no fear in love, but perfect love casts out fear" (1 Jn 4:18).

The Church rereads the message of mercy in order to bring with greater effectiveness to this generation at the end of the millennium and to future generations *the light of hope.* Unceasingly, the Church implores from God mercy for everyone.

"At no time and in no historical period – especially at a moment as critical as our own – can the Church forget *the prayer that is a cry for the mercy of God* amid the many forms of evil which weigh upon humanity and threaten it....

"The more the human conscience succumbs to secularization, loses its sense of the very meaning of the word 'mercy,' moves away from God, and distances itself from the mystery of mercy, the more *the Church has the right and the duty* to appeal to the God of mercy 'with loud cries'" (*Dives in Misericordia,* #15).

Precisely for this reason, this shrine, too, has found a place on my pilgrim itinerary. I come here to commend the concerns of the Church and of humanity to the merciful Christ. On the threshold of the third millennium *I come to entrust to Him once more my Petrine ministry – "Jesus, I trust in you!"*

The message of Divine Mercy has always been near and dear to me. It is as if history had inscribed it in the tragic experience of the Second World War. In those difficult years it was *a particular support and an inexhaustible source of hope*, not only for the people of Kraków but for the entire nation.

This was also my personal experience, which I took with me to the See of Peter and which, in a sense, forms the image of this Pontificate.

I give thanks to divine Providence that I have been enabled to contribute personally to the fulfillment of Christ's will, through the institution of the Feast of Divine Mercy. Here, near relics of Blessed Faustina Kowalska, I give thanks also for the gift of her beatification. I pray unceasingly that God will have "mercy on us and on the whole world" [From The Chaplet of Divine Mercy, *Diary,* 476].

"Blessed are the merciful, for they shall obtain mercy" (Mt 5:7).

Dear Sisters! An extraordinary vocation is yours. Choosing from among you Blessed Faustina, Christ has made your congregation the guardian of this place, and at the same time He has called you to a particular apostolate, that of His mercy. I ask you: accept this responsibility!

The people of today need your *proclamation of mercy:* they need your *works of mercy* and they need your *prayer to obtain mercy* [cf *Diary*, 742].

Do not neglect any of these dimensions of the apostolate. Fulfill it in union with the Archbishop of Kraków, to whose heart is so dear the devotion to The Divine Mercy, and in union with the whole ecclesial community over which he presides.

May this shared work bear much fruit! May The Divine Mercy transform people's hearts! May this shrine, known already in many parts of the world, become a center of worship of The Divine Mercy which shines on the whole Church! ...

I cordially bless all who are present here and all those devoted to The Divine Mercy.

Regina Caeli, Divine Mercy Sunday: April 19, 1998

Accept Divine Mercy with an open heart

L'Osservatore Romano, April 22, 1998

On 19 April, the Second Sunday of Easter, the Holy Father led the recitation of the Regina Caeli, which he introduced with a reflection on the Lord's merciful love and on the Special Synod for Asia.

Dear Brothers and Sisters,

1. In today's Gospel passage we read that Jesus appeared to the Apostles in the Upper Room and said to them: "Receive the Holy Spirit. If you forgive the sins of any, they are forgiven; if you retain the sins of any, they are retained" (Jn 20:22-23). With these words, the Risen Christ calls the Apostles to be messengers and ministers of His merciful love and from that day, from generation to generation, this proclamation of hope has resounded in the heart of the Church for every believer. Blessed are those who open their hearts to Divine Mercy! The Lord's merciful love precedes and accompanies every act of evangelization and enriches it with extraordinary fruits of conversion and spiritual renewal.

2. In every corner of the world, the way of the Christian people is marked by the constant action of Divine Mercy. This happened in the early communities and likewise in the Church's later developments on the various continents.

Today our attention is focused in particular on the signs of mercy which God worked and continues to work in Asia. In fact, this morning's solemn Eucharistic celebration in St. Peter's Basilica opened the Special Assembly for Asia of the Synod of Bishops.

The theme chosen for this Synod Assembly is "Jesus Christ the Savior and His Mission of Love and Service in Asia: 'that they may have life, and have it abundantly' (Jn 10:10)". This is a most appropriate theme for Asia, especially in view of its many religions and cultures, its variety of economic and political situations. It is an enormous land, open to the proclamation of salvation in Jesus Christ and to the witness of Christian solidarity towards peoples who are often sorely tried. At this time, I am thinking particularly of the peoples of North Korea, exhausted by hunger and hardship: as I urge the Church's charitable organizations to take responsibility for this difficult situation, I hope that the international community will also provide the necessary assistance.

3. Let us entrust to Mary, Mother of the Church, the work of the Special Assembly for Asia of the Synod of Bishops. May she, who was at the heart of the apostolic community as a teacher of prayer and communion, obtain an abundant outpouring of the Holy Spirit on the Synod Fathers and on all the Christian communities throughout the Asian continent. May Our Lady, Mother of Divine Mercy, also enable us to accept with open hearts the gift of merciful love that the Risen Christ offers all believers, so that His mercy and His peace may mark the present and the future of all humanity.

Regina Caeli, Divine Mercy Sunday, April 11, 1999:

Silence the arms and return to dialogue

L'Osservatore Romano, April 14, 1999

On Sunday, 11 April, the Octave of Easter and Divine Mercy Sunday, the Holy Father led the recitation of the Regina Caeli, which he introduced with a reflection on God's merciful love, drawing attention to the glaring contrast between the suffering caused by the war in the Balkans and the Risen Christ's gift of mercy and peace. The Pope asked the faithful to intensify their prayers for an end to the war and for peaceful coexistence among all the peoples of that region.

Dear Brothers and Sisters,

1. At the end of the Octave of Easter, with a special thought for our Orthodox brothers and sisters who are celebrating this solemnity today, I make my own the words of the Apostle Peter, proclaimed in the liturgy: "Blessed be the God and Father of our Lord Jesus Christ! By His great mercy we have been born anew to a living hope through the resurrection of Jesus Christ from the dead" (1 Pt 1:3). On their way to the Jubilee, the entire People of God raise a hymn of thanksgiving to God the Father who, in Christ's Paschal Mystery, revealed to the world His face and, so to speak, His heart "rich in mercy" (Eph 2:4).

This Sunday is also called Divine Mercy Sunday: in this year dedicated to God the Father, it is an excellent occasion to enter into the authentic Jubilee spirit as individuals and as the Church, in accordance with Jesus' own words: "The Spirit of the Lord is upon me, because He has sent Me ... to announce a year of favor from the Lord" (Lk 4: 18-19). I am very pleased that many priests and faithful have gathered this morning in St. Peter's Square for a solemn Eucharist celebrated by Cardinal Fiorenzo Angelini, whom I cordially greet, and with him everyone present, as I express my pleasure with your devotion to the merciful Jesus.

I warmly encourage you to be apostles of Divine Mercy, like Blessed Faustina Kowalska, wherever you live and work.

2. How could we not note the glaring contrast between the invitation to mercy and forgiveness echoing in today's liturgy and the violence of the tragic conflicts which are soaking the Balkan region in blood? May peace prevail at last! Here I renew the appeal dictated not only by faith, but first of all by reason: may people be able to live together in harmony in their lands; may weapons be silenced and dialogue resumed!

My thoughts turn constantly to those who are suffering the

harsh consequences of the war and I pray the Risen Lord, the Prince of Peace, to give us the gift of His peace.

3. I would like to invite all believers to intensify their prayer for peace, because God offers what sometimes seems almost humanly impossible to those who request it as a gift of His mercy.

For this reason, let us invoke the intercession of Blessed Mary, Mother of Mercy. We pray to you to help us set out courageously on the way of love and peace.

Universal Prayer: Confession of Sins and Asking for Forgiveness, March 12, 2000

Introduction

The Holy Father: Brothers and Sisters, let us turn with trust to God our Father, who is merciful and compassionate, slow to anger, great in love and fidelity, and ask Him to accept the repentance of His people who humbly confess their sins, and to grant them mercy. [All pray for a moment in silence.]

I. CONFESSION OF SINS IN GENERAL

Cardinal Bernardin Gantin: Let us pray that our confession and repentance will be inspired by the Holy Spirit, that our sorrow will be conscious and deep, and that, humbly viewing the sins of the past in an authentic "purification of memory", we will be committed to the path of true conversion. [Silent prayer.] **The Holy Father:** Lord God, Your pilgrim Church, which You ever sanctify in the blood of Your Son, counts among her children in every age members whose holiness shines brightly forth and members whose disobedience to You contradicts the faith we profess and the Holy Gospel. You, who remain ever faithful, even when we are unfaithful, forgive our sins and grant that we may bear true witness to You before all men and women. We ask this through Christ our Lord. R. Amen. Cantor: Kyrie, eleison; Kyrie, eleison; Kyrie, eleison.

The assembly repeats: Kyrie, eleison; Kyrie, eleison; Kyrie, eleison. [A lamp is lit before the Crucifix.]

II. CONFESSION OF SINS COMMITTED IN THE SERVICE OF TRUTH

Cardinal Joseph Ratzinger: Let us pray that each one of us, looking to the Lord Jesus, meek and humble of heart, will recognize that even men of the Church, in the name of faith and morals, have sometimes used methods not in keeping with the Gospel in the solemn duty of defending the truth. [Silent prayer.] **The Holy Father:** Lord, God of all men and women, in certain periods of history Christians have, at times, given in to intolerance and have not been faithful to the great commandment of love, sullying in this way the face of the Church, your Spouse. Have mercy on your sinful children and accept our resolve to seek and promote truth in the gentleness of charity, in the firm knowledge that truth can prevail only in virtue of truth itself. We ask this through Christ our Lord. R. Amen. R. Kyrie, eleison; Kyrie, eleison; Kyrie, eleison. [A lamp is lit before the Crucifix.]

III. CONFESSION OF SINS WHICH HAVE HARMED THE UNITY OF THE BODY OF CHRIST

Cardinal Roger Etchegaray: Let us pray that our recognition of the sins which have rent the unity of the Body of Christ and wounded fraternal charity will facilitate the way to reconciliation and communion among all Christians. [Silent prayer.] **The Holy Father:** Merciful Father, on the night before His Passion, Your Son prayed for the unity of those who believe in Him: in disobedience to His will, however, believers have opposed one another, becoming divided, and have mutually condemned one another and fought against one another. We urgently implore Your forgiveness and we beseech the gift of a repentant heart, so that all Christians, reconciled with You and with one another will be able, in one body and in one spirit, to experience anew the joy of full communion. We ask this through Christ our Lord. R. Amen. R. Kyrie, eleison; Kyrie, eleison; Kyrie, eleison. [A lamp is lit before the Crucifix.]

IV. CONFESSION OF SINS AGAINST THE PEOPLE OF ISRAEL

Cardinal Edward Cassidy: Let us pray that, in recalling the sufferings endured by the people of Israel throughout history, Christians will acknowledge the sins committed by not a few of their number against the people of the Covenant and the blessings, and in this way will purify their hearts. [Silent prayer.] The **Holy Father:** God of our fathers, You chose Abraham and his descendants to bring your Name to the Nations: we are deeply saddened by the behavior of those who in the course of history have caused these children of Yours to suffer, and asking Your forgiveness, we wish to commit ourselves to genuine brotherhood with the people of the Covenant. We ask this through Christ our Lord. R. Amen. R. Kyrie, eleison; Kyrie, eleison; Kyrie eleison. [A lamp is lit before the Crucifix.]

V. CONFESSION OF SINS COMMITTED IN ACTIONS AGAINST LOVE, PEACE, THE RIGHTS OF PEOPLES, AND RESPECT FOR CULTURES AND RELIGIONS

Archbishop Stephen Fumio Hamao: Let us pray that contemplating Jesus, our Lord and our Peace, Christians will be able to repent of the words and attitudes caused by pride, by hatred, by the desire to dominate others, by enmity towards members of other religions and towards the weakest groups in society, such as immigrants and itinerants. [Silent prayer.] The **Holy Father:** Lord of the world, Father of all, through Your Son You asked us to love our enemies, to do good to those who hate us and to pray for those who persecute us. Yet Christians have often denied the Gospel; yielding to a mentality of power, they have violated the rights of ethnic groups and peoples, and shown contempt for their cultures and religious traditions: be patient and merciful towards us, and grant us Your forgiveness! We ask this through Christ our Lord. R. Amen. R. Kyrie, eleison; Kyrie, eleison; Kyrie, eleison. [A lamp is lit before the Crucifix.]

VI. CONFESSION OF SINS AGAINST THE DIGNITY OF WOMEN AND THE UNITY OF THE HUMAN RACE

Cardinal Francis Arinze: Let us pray for all those who have suffered offences against their human dignity and whose rights have been trampled; let us pray for women, who are all too often humiliated and marginalized, and let us acknowledge the forms of acquiescence in these sins of which Christians too have been guilty. [Silent prayer.] **The Holy Father:** Lord God, our Father, You created the human being, man and woman, in Your image and likeness and you willed the diversity of peoples within the unity of the human family. At times, however, the equality of Your sons and daughters has not been acknowledged, and Christians have been guilty of attitudes of rejection and exclusion, consenting to acts of discrimination on the basis of racial and ethnic differences. Forgive us and grant us the grace to heal the wounds still present in Your community on account of sin, so that we will all feel ourselves to be Your sons and daughters. We ask this through Christ our Lord. R. Amen. R. Kyrie, eleison; Kyrie, eleison; Kyrie, eleison. [A lamp is lit before the Crucifix.]

VII. CONFESSION OF SINS IN RELATION TO THE FUNDAMENTAL RIGHTS OF THE PERSON

Archbishop Francois Xavier Nguyen Van Thuan: Let us pray for all the men and women of the world, especially for minors who are victims of abuse, for the poor, the alienated, the disadvantaged; let us pray for those who are most defenseless, the unborn killed in their mother's womb or even exploited for experimental purposes by those who abuse the promise of biotechnology and distort the aims of science. [Silent prayer.] **The Holy Father:** God, our Father, You always hear the cry of the poor. How many times have Christians themselves not recognized You in the hungry, the thirsty and the naked, in the persecuted, the imprisoned, and in those incapable of defending themselves, especially in the first stages of life. For all those who have committed acts of injustice by trusting in wealth and power and showing contempt for the "little ones" who are so dear to You, we ask Your forgiveness. Have mercy on us and accept our repentance. We ask this through Christ our Lord. R. Amen. R. Kyrie, eleison; Kyrie, eleison; Kyrie, eleison. [A lamp is lit before the Crucifix.]

Concluding Prayer

The Holy Father: Most merciful Father, Your Son, Jesus Christ, the judge of the living and the dead, in the humility of His first coming redeemed humanity from sin and in His glorious return He will demand an account of every sin. Grant that our forebears, our brothers and sisters, and we, Your servants, who by the grace of the Holy Spirit turn back to You in whole-hearted repentance, may experience Your mercy and receive the forgiveness of our sins. We ask this through Christ our Lord. R. Amen.

[As a sign of penance and veneration the Holy Father embraces and kisses the Crucifix.]

ANGELUS: "DAY OF PARDON", Sunday, March 12, 2000

(This text was taken from the Internet, Vatican Web-site)

Dear Brothers and Sisters!

1. In the faith context of the Great Jubilee, today we are celebrating the Day of Pardon. This morning in St. Peter's Basilica, I presided at a moving and solemn penitential act. On this First Sunday of Lent, Bishops and Ecclesial Communities in various parts of the world knelt before God, in the name of the entire Christian people, to implore His forgiveness.

The Holy Year is a time of purification: the Church is holy because Christ is her Head and her Spouse; the Spirit is her life-giving soul; the Virgin Mary and the saints are her most authentic expression. However, the children of the Church know the experience of sin, whose shadows are cast over her, obscuring her beauty. For this reason the Church does not cease to implore God's forgiveness for the sins of her members.

2. This is not a judgment on the subjective responsibility of our brothers and sisters who have gone before us: judgment belongs to God alone, who - unlike us human beings - "sees the heart and the mind" (cf Jer 20: 12). Today's act is a sincere recognition of the sins committed by the Church's children in the distant and recent past, and a humble plea for God's forgiveness. This will reawaken consciences, enabling Christians to enter the third millennium with greater openness to God and His plan of love.

As we ask forgiveness, let us also forgive. This is what we say every day when we recite the prayer Jesus taught us: "Our Father ... forgive us our trespasses as we forgive those who trespass against us" (Mt 6: 12). For all believers, may the fruit of this Jubilee Day be forgiveness reciprocally given and received!

Reconciliation springs from forgiveness. This is our hope for every Ecclesial Community, for all believers in Christ and for the whole world.

3. Forgiven and ready to forgive, Christians enter the third millennium as more credible witnesses to hope. After centuries marked by violence and destruction, especially the last tragic one, the Church offers humanity, as it crosses the threshold of the third millennium, the Gospel of forgiveness and reconciliation, a prerequisite for building genuine peace.

To be witnesses to hope! This is also the theme of the Spiritual Exercises which I will begin this evening with my collaborators in the Roman Curia. For now, I thank all who wish to accompany me in prayer, and I call upon Our Lady, Mother of Divine Mercy, to help everyone to observe the Lenten season fruitfully.

HOMILY OF THE HOLY FATHER

MASS IN ST. PETER'S SQUARE FOR THE CANON-IZATION OF SISTER MARIA FAUSTINA KOWALSKA

Sunday, April 30, 2000

1. "Confitemini Domino quoniam bonus, quoniam in saeculum misericordia eius"; "Give thanks to the Lord for He is good; His steadfast love endures forever" (Ps 118:1). So the Church sings on the Octave of Easter, as if receiving from Christ's lips these words of the Psalm; from the lips of the Risen Christ, who bears the great message of Divine Mercy and entrusts its ministry to the Apostles in the Upper Room: "Peace be with you. As the Father has sent Me, even so I send you.... Receive the Holy Spirit. If you forgive the sins of any, they are forgiven; if you retain the sins of any, they are retained" (Jn 20:21-23).

Before speaking these words, Jesus shows His hands and His side. He points, that is, to the wounds of the Passion, especially the wound in His heart, the source from which flows the great wave of mercy poured out on humanity. From that heart, Sister Faustina Kowalska, the blessed whom from now on we will call a saint, will see two rays of light shining from that heart and illuminating the world. "The two rays", Jesus Himself explained to her one day, "represent blood and water" (Diary, Libreria Editrice Vaticana, p.132).

2. Blood and water! We immediately think of the testimony given by the Evangelist John, who, when a soldier on Calvary pierced Christ's side with his spear, sees blood and water flowing from it (cf Jn 19:34). Moreover, if the blood recalls the sacrifice of the Cross and the gift of the Eucharist, the water, in Johannine symbolism, represents not only Baptism but also the gift of the Holy Spirit (cf Jn 3:5; 4:14; 7:37-39).

Divine Mercy reaches human beings through the heart of Christ crucified. "My daughter, say that I am love and mercy personified", Jesus will ask Sister Faustina (Diary, p. 374). Christ pours out this mercy on humanity through the sending of the Spirit who, in the Trinity, is the Person-Love. And is not mercy love's "second name" (cf. Dives in Misericordia, #7), understood in its deepest and most tender aspect, in its ability to take upon itself the burden of any need and, especially, in its immense capacity for forgiveness?

Today my joy is truly great in presenting the life and witness of Sister Faustina Kowalska to the whole Church as a gift of God for our time. By divine Providence, the life of this humble daughter of Poland was completely linked with the history of the 20th century, the century we have just left behind. In fact, it was between the First and Second World Wars that Christ entrusted His message of mercy to her. Those who remember, who were witnesses and participants in the events of those years and the horrible sufferings they caused for millions of people, know well how necessary was the message of mercy.

Jesus told Sister Faustina: "Humanity will not find peace until it turns trustfully to Divine Mercy" (Diary, p. 132). Through the work of the Polish religious, this message has become linked forever to the 20th century, the last of the second millennium and the bridge to the third. It is not a new message, but can be considered a gift of special enlightenment that helps us to relive the Gospel of Easter more intensely, to offer it as a ray of light to the men and women of our time.

3. What will the years ahead bring us? What will man's future on earth be like? We are not given to know. However, it is certain that, in addition to new progress, there will unfortunately be no lack of painful experiences. But the light of Divine Mercy, which the Lord in a way wished to return to the world through Sister Faustina's charism, will illumine the way for the men and women of the third millennium.

However, as the Apostles once did, today too humanity must welcome into the upper room of history the Risen Christ, who shows the wounds of His Crucifixion and repeats "Peace be with you!". Humanity must let itself be touched and pervaded by the Spirit given to it by the Risen Christ. It is the Spirit who heals the wounds of the heart, pulls down the barriers that separate us from God and divide us from one another, and at the same time, restores the joy of the Father's love and of fraternal unity.

4. It is important then that we accept the whole message that comes to us from the Word of God on this Second Sunday of Easter, which from now on throughout the Church will be called "Divine Mercy Sunday". In the various readings, the liturgy seems to indicate the path of mercy which, while re-establishing the relationship of each person with God, also creates new relations of fraternal solidarity among human beings. Christ has taught us that "man not only receives and experiences the mercy of God, but is also called to 'practice mercy' towards others: 'Blessed are the merciful, for they shall obtain mercy' " (Mt 5:7) (Dives in Misericordia, #14). He also showed us the many paths of mercy, which not only forgive sins but reach out to all human needs. Jesus bent over every kind of human poverty, material and spiritual.

His message of mercy continues to reach us through His hands held out to suffering man. This is how Sister Faustina saw Him and proclaimed Him to people on all the continents when, hidden in her convent at Łagiewniki in Kraków, she made her life a hymn to mercy; Misericordias Domini in aeternum cantabo.

5. Sister Faustina's canonization has a particular eloquence. By this act I intend today to pass this message on to the new millennium. I pass it on to all people, so that they will learn to know ever better the true face of God and the true face of their brethren.

In fact, love of God and love of one's brothers and sisters are inseparable, as the First Letter of John has reminded us: "By this we know that we love the children of God, when we love God and obey His commandments"(5:2). Here the Apostle reminds us of the truth of love, showing us its measure and criterion in the observance of the commandments.

It is not easy to love with a deep love, which lies in the authentic gift of self. This love can only be learned by penetrating the mystery of God's love. Looking at him, being one with His fatherly heart, we are able to look with new eyes at our brothers and sisters, with an attitude of unselfishness and solidarity, of generosity and forgiveness. All this is mercy!

To the extent that humanity penetrates the mystery of this merciful gaze, it will seem possible to fulfill the ideal we heard in today's first reading. "The community of believers were of one heart and one mind. None of them ever claimed anything as his own; rather everything was held in common" (Acts 4:32). Here mercy gave form to human relations and community life; it constituted the basis for the sharing of goods. This led to the spiritual and corporal "works of mercy". Here mercy became a concrete way of being "neighbor" to one's neediest brothers and sisters.

6. Sister Faustina Kowalska wrote in her Diary: "I feel tremendous pain when I see the sufferings of my neighbors. All my neighbors' sufferings reverberate in my own heart; I carry their anguish in my heart in such a way that it even physically destroys me. I would like all their sorrows to fall upon me, in order to relieve my neighbor" (Diary, p. 365). This is the degree of compassion to which love leads, when it takes the love of God as its measure!

It is this love which must inspire humanity today, if it is to face the crisis of the meaning of life, the challenges of the most diverse needs and, especially, the duty to defend the dignity of every human person. Thus the message of Divine Mercy is also implicitly a message about the value of every human being. Each person is precious in God's eyes; Christ gave His life for each one; to everyone the Father gives His Spirit and offers intimacy.

7. This consoling message is addressed above all to those who, afflicted by a particularly harsh trial or crushed by the weight of the sins they committed, have lost all confidence in life and are tempted to give in to despair. To them the gentle face of Christ is offered; those rays from His heart touch them and shine upon them, warm them, show them the way and fill them with hope. How many souls have been consoled by the prayer "Jesus, I trust in you", which Providence intimated through Sister Faustina! This simple act of abandonment to Jesus dispels the thickest clouds and lets a ray of light penetrate every life. Jezu, ufam tobie!

8. Misericordias Domini in aeternum cantabo (Ps 88 [89]:2). Let us too, the pilgrim Church, join our voice to the voice of Mary most holy, "Mother of Mercy"; to the voice of this new saint who sings of mercy with all God's friends in the heavenly Jerusalem.

And you, Faustina, a gift of God to our time, a gift from the land of Poland to the whole Church, obtain for us an awareness of the depth of Divine Mercy. Help us to have a living experience of it and to bear witness to it among our brothers and sisters. May your message of light and hope spread throughout the world, spurring sinners to conversion, calming rivalries and hatred and opening individuals and nations to the practice of brotherhood. Today, fixing our gaze with you on the face of the Risen Christ, let us make our own your prayer of trusting abandonment and say with firm hope: Christ Jesus, I trust in you! Jezu, ufam tobie!

Regina Caeli, Divine Mercy Sunday, April 30, 2000:
Canonization of St. Faustina

L'Osservatore Romano, May 3, 2000

Before imparting the final blessing of the Mass he celebrated on Sunday, 30 April, for the canonization of Sr. Mary Faustina Kowalska, the Holy Father led the recitation of the Regina Caeli prayer, which he introduced with greetings in various languages to the pilgrims in St. Peter's Square and those at the Shrine of Divine Mercy in Krakow-Lagiewniki, Poland, who were linked by television with the celebration in Rome.

1. At the close of this celebration, in which our Easter joy is combined with that of Sister Faustina Kowalska's canonization, I affectionately greet and thank all of you who have come from various parts of the world. I ardently hope that each of you can experience what Our Lady one day assured Saint Faustina: "I am not only the Queen of Heaven, but also the Mother of Mercy and your Mother" (Diary, 141).

2. The message of Divine Mercy and the image of the merciful Christ of which Sister Faustina Kowalska speaks to us today are a vivid expression of the spirit of the Great Jubilee which the whole Church is celebrating with joy and fruitfulness. Many of you have come to honor the new saint. May her intercession bring abundant gifts of repentance, forgiveness and renewed spiritual vitality to the Church in your countries. May the thought of God's loving kindness stir up in your hearts new energies for works of faith and Christian solidarity.

I cordially greet the French-speaking pilgrims, especially those who have taken part in the canonization of Sister Faustina. Following her example, may you entrust yourselves totally to the Lord and praise Him in the power of His mercy! May the renewing strength of the Risen Christ fill your hearts!

At the same time my thoughts embrace all my compatriots and I entrust them to the intercession of the saintly Sister

Faustina. In the new millennium, may the message of the merciful love of God, who bends over all human poverty, be an endless source of hope for everyone and a call to show active love to one's brothers and sisters. I cordially bless you all.

Today we also join the Primate, Archbishop of Gniezno, and all our compatriots who have gathered in Gniezno for the solemnity of Saint Adalbert.

"Gaude Mater Poloniae...". Rejoice, Mother of Poland; rejoice, Sisters of Our Lady of Mercy, because our Sister Faustina has been raised to the glory of the saints.

I cordially greet the pilgrims from Poland and all those devoted to the Divine Mercy who have gathered at the shrine in Kraków-Lagiewniki. I am happy that on this day - so special for our country - representatives of the Government of the Republic of Poland are here with the Prime Minister, as well as representatives of Solidarnosc.

Divine Providence has linked Sister Faustina's life with the cities of Warsaw, Plock, Vilnius and Kraków. Today I recall the names of these cities, of which the new saint is the patroness, entrusting to their residents a particular concern for the Divine Mercy apostolate.

3. And now let us pray to the merciful Queen of Heaven.

Evening Prayer, Divine Mercy Sunday, April 30, 2000

L'Osservatore Romano, May 3, 2000

On Sunday, 30 April, at the close of the prayer service that is held each evening of the Jubilee in St. Peter's Square, the Holy Father came to the window of his study and greeted the pilgrims gathered in front of the basilica.

I am pleased to extend a cordial greeting to the pilgrims attending the prayer that is celebrated each evening in St. Peter's Square during the Jubilee.

Dear brothers and sisters, on this Second Sunday of Easter, on which I had the joy of enrolling Sister Faustina Kowalska, Apostle of Divine Mercy, among the saints, I urge you always to trust in God's merciful love revealed to us in Christ Jesus, who died and rose again for our salvation. May the personal experience of this love commit everyone to becoming, in turn, a witness of active charity towards his brothers and sisters. Make Sister Faustina's beautiful exclamation your own: "Jesus, I trust in you!".

My Blessing to all!

[The Holy Father then said in Polish:]

I cordially greet all who have gathered on this special day in St. Peter's Square to thank God at evening prayer for the gift of Sister Faustina's canonization. With all my heart I join you in this thanksgiving.

May you always remember the Divine Mercy Sunday of the year 2000. I pray God that this memory may increase in all hearts a firm trust in His gracious love and strengthen them on the paths of the third millennium. *Jesus, I trust in you!*

May God, rich in mercy, bless you and your loved ones.

Proclamation of Divine Mercy Sunday

By virtue of a Decree issued on May 5, 2000 by the Congregation for Divine Worship and the Discipline of the Sacraments, the Holy See proclaimed the Second Sunday of Easter also as Divine Mercy Sunday.

Decree

Merciful and gracious is the Lord (Ps 111:4), who, out of great love with which He loved us (Eph 2:4) and [out of] unspeakable goodness, gave us his Only-begotten Son as our Redeemer, so that through the Death and Resurrection of this Son He might open the way to eternal life for the human race, and that the adopted children who receive his mercy within his temple might lift up his praise to the ends of the earth.

In our times, the Christian faithful in many parts of the world wish to praise that divine mercy in divine worship, particularly in the celebration of the Paschal Mystery, in which God's loving kindness especially shines forth.

Acceding to these wishes, the Supreme Pontiff John Paul II has graciously determined that in the Roman Missal, after the title "Second Sunday of Easter," there shall henceforth be added the appellation "(or *Divine Mercy Sunday*)", and has prescribed that the texts assigned for that day in the same Missal and the Liturgy of the Hours of the Roman Rite are always to be used for the liturgical celebration of this Sunday.

The Congregation for Divine Worship and the Discipline of the Sacraments now publishes these decisions of the Supreme Pontiff so that they may take effect.

Anything to the contrary notwithstanding.

> Cardinal Jorge A. Medina Esteves
> Prefect
> +Francesco Pio Tamburrino
> Archbishop Secretary

Pope's Homily on Divine Mercy Sunday, April 22, 2001

"This Miracle ... Has Changed Humanity's Destiny"

VATICAN CITY, APR. 29, 2001- A year after the canonization of Sister Faustina Kowalska, a Polish religious known as the apostle of Divine Mercy, John Paul II celebrated the Mass of the Divine Mercy in St Peter's Square on April 22. Here is a translation of his homily, which was given in Italian.

1. "Fear not, I am the first and the last, and the living one; I died, and behold I am alive for evermore" (Rv1:17-18).

We heard these comforting words in the Second Reading taken from the Book of Revelation. They invite us to turn our gaze to Christ, to experience his reassuring presence. To each person, whatever his condition, even if it were the most complicated and dramatic, the Risen One repeats: "Fear not!"; I died on the Cross but now "I am alive for evermore"; "I am the first and the last, and the living one".

"The first," that is, the source of every being and the first fruits of the new creation; "the last," the definitive end of history; "the living one," the inexhaustible source of life that triumphed over death for ever. In the Messiah, crucified and risen, we recognize the features of the Lamb sacrificed on Golgotha, who implores forgiveness for his torturers and opens the gates of heaven to repentant sinners; we glimpse the face of the immortal King who now has "the keys of Death and Hades" (Rv 1:18).

2. "Give thanks to the Lord, for he is good; for his mercy endures for ever!" (Ps 117: 1).

Let us make our own the Psalmist's exclamation which we sang in the Responsorial Psalm: The Lord's mercy endures for ever! In order to understand thoroughly the truth of these words, let us be led by the liturgy to the heart of the event of salvation, which unites Christ's Death and Resurrection with our lives and with the world's history. This miracle of mercy has radically changed humanity's destiny. It is a miracle in which is unfolded the fullness of the love of the Father who, for our redemption, does not even draw back before the sacrifice of his Only-begotten Son.

In the humiliated and suffering Christ, believers and non-believers can admire a surprising solidarity, which binds him to our human condition beyond all imaginable measure. The Cross, even after the Resurrection of the Son of God, "speaks and never ceases to speak of God the Father, who is absolutely faithful to his eternal love for man.... Believing in this love means believing in mercy" (Dives in Misericordia, n. 7).

Let us thank the Lord for his love, which is stronger than death and sin. It is revealed and put into practice as mercy in our daily lives, and prompts every person in turn to have "mercy" towards the Crucified One. Is not loving God and loving one's neighbour and even one's "enemies", after Jesus' example, the programme of life of every baptized person and of the whole Church?

3. With these sentiments we are celebrating the Second Sunday of Easter, which since last year, the year of the Great Jubilee, is also called "Divine Mercy Sunday". It is a great joy for me to be able to join all of you, dear pilgrims and faithful who have come from various nations to commemorate, after one year, the canonization of Sr. Faustina Kowalska, witness and messenger of the Lord's merciful love. The elevation to the honours of the altar of this humble religious, a daughter of my land, is not only a gift for Poland but for all humanity. Indeed the message she brought is the appropriate and incisive answer that God wanted to offer to the questions and expectations of human beings in our time, marked by terrible tragedies. Jesus said to Sr. Faustina one day: "Humanity will never find peace until it turns with trust to Divine Mercy" (Diary, p.132). Divine Mercy! This is the Easter gift that the Church receives from the risen Christ and offers to humanity at the dawn of the third millennium.

4. The Gospel, which has just been proclaimed, helps us to grasp the full sense and value of this gift. The Evangelist John makes us share in the emotion felt by the Apostles in their meeting with Christ after his Resurrection. Our attention focuses on the gesture of the Master, who transmits to the fearful, astounded disciples the mission of being ministers of Divine Mercy. He shows them his hands and his side, which bear the marks of the Passion, and tells them: "As the Father has sent me, even so I send you" (Jn 20: 21). Immediately afterwards "he breathed on

them, and said to them, "Receive the Holy Spirit. If you forgive the sins of any, they are forgiven; if you retain the sins of any, they are retained' "(Jn 20: 22-23). Jesus entrusted to them the gift of "forgiving sins", a gift that flows from the wounds in his hands, his feet, and especially from his pierced side. From there a wave of mercy is poured out over all humanity.

Let us relive this moment with great spiritual intensity. Today the Lord also shows us his glorious wounds and his heart, an inexhaustible source of light and truth, of love and forgiveness.

5. The Heart of Christ! His "Sacred Heart" has given men everything: redemption, salvation, sanctification. St. Faustina Kowalska saw coming from this Heart that was overflowing with generous love, two rays of light which illuminated the world. "The two rays", according to what Jesus himself told her, "represent the blood and the water" (Diary, p. 132). The blood recalls the sacrifice of Golgotha and the mystery of the Eucharist; the water, according to the rich symbolism of the Evangelist John, makes us think of Baptism and the Gift of the Holy Spirit (cf. Jn 3: 5; 4: 14).

Through the mystery of this wounded heart, the restorative tide of God's merciful love continues to spread over the men and women of our time. Here alone can those who long for true and lasting happiness find its secret.

6. "Jesus, I trust in you". This prayer, dear to so many of the devout, clearly expresses the attitude with which we too would like to abandon ourselves trustfully in your hands, O Lord, our only Saviour.

You are burning with the desire to be loved and those in tune with the sentiments of your heart learn how to build the new civilization of love. A simple act of abandonment is enough to overcome the barriers of darkness and sorrow, of doubt and desperation. The rays of your divine mercy restore hope, in a special way, to those who feel overwhelmed by the burden of sin.

Mary, Mother of Mercy, help us always to have this trust in your Son, our Redeemer. Help us too, St. Faustina, whom we remember today with special affection. Fixing our weak gaze on the divine Saviour's face, we would like to repeat with you: "Jesus, I trust in you". Now and for ever. Amen.

[translation by *L'Osservatore Romano*]

Regina Caeli: April 22, 2001

Our Lady exemplifies God's mercy

After celebrating Mass on Divine Mercy Sunday, 22 April, almost a year after Sr Faustina Kowalska's canonization, the Holy Father introduced the prayer of the Regina Caeli for the faithful in St Peter's Square with a short reflection on the spiritual motherhood of the Blessed Virgin.

1. As we approach the conclusion of the solemn Eucharistic celebration, let us turn our gaze to Mary Most Holy, whom we call upon today with the sweetest name of "Mater misericordiae." Mary is "Mother of mercy," because she is the Mother of Jesus in whom God revealed to the world his "heart" overflowing with love.

God's compassion for man is communicated to the world precisely through the Virgin Mary's motherhood. Mary's motherhood, which began in Nazareth through the work of the Holy Spirit, was fulfilled in the Easter mystery, when she was closely associated with the Passion, Death and Resurrection of the divine Son. At the foot of the Cross Our Lady became mother of the disciples of Christ, mother of the Church and of all humanity. "Mater misericordiae."

2. I greet the pilgrims who have come here from Poland, and all who have a special devotion to God's mercy and have taken part in this Holy Mass by radio and television. In a special way I have joined in spirit the Cardinal of Krakow and the vast num-

ber of Bishops, religious and faithful who have gathered today at the Shrine of Divine Mercy in Lagiewniki. During this celebration together with you I thanked God who almost a year ago granted me the grace to canonize Sr. Faustina Kowalska, the chosen apostle of the merciful Christ, and to proclaim the Second Sunday of Easter as the feast of Divine Mercy for the entire Church.

Filled with joy we present ourselves before the Risen One today and say with faith: "Jesus, I trust in you!" May this confession full of love strengthen everyone on the path of daily life and encourage them to undertake works of mercy for their brothers and sisters. May this be a message of hope for the entire new millennium.

3. Now, with the recitation of the antiphon "Regina Caeli," we ask Mary to enable us to experience the deep joy of the Resurrection and to collaborate with dedication in the universal plan of Divine Mercy.

John Paul II, The Mercy Pope
Chronology of Mercy Events challenging us to be merciful.

1942 Karol Wojtyla enters the clandestine seminary in Krakow. During this time Andrew Deskur, now retired Cardinal in the Vatican, introduces him to the message of Divine Mercy, revealed to the mystic nun, now Saint Faustina Kowalska (1905-1938).

1958 Bishop Karol Wojtyla often visited the motherhouse of the Sisters of Our Lady of Mercy, where Sister Faustina died and was buried. He came for his own time of retreat and to conduct retreats for the Sisters (verbally related in 1989 by Mother Pauline, superior general).

Oct. 1965 Archbishop Karol Wojtyla of Krakow confers with Cardinal Ottaviani about the desire of the faithful in Poland to have Sister Faustina raised to the honors of the altar, despite a notification from the Vatican prohibiting "the spread of images and writings that propose the devotion of The Divine Mercy in the form proposed by the same Sister Faustina."

Oct. 21, 1965 Twenty-seven years after the death of Sister Faustina, Bishop Julian Groblicki, specially delegated by Archbishop Karol Wojtyla, begins with a solemn session, in the Archdiocese of Krakow, the Informative Process relating to the life and virtues of Sister Faustina. From this moment, Sister Faustina is worthy of the title "Servant of God."

June 26, 1967 Archbishop Karol Wojtyla becomes Karol Cardinal Wojtyla.

Sept. 20, 1967 The Archbishop of Krakow, Karol Cardinal Wojtyla officially closes the first informative stage in the process for the beatification of the Servant of God, Sister Faustina Kowalska.

The outcome of the Process of Information shows that the action in Rome with regard to Sister Faustina was taken (at the least) on insufficient evidence. (Official communications between Rome and the Church in Poland during those post-war years, especially with regard to religious matters, were very difficult. Relevant, authentic documents could not be made available to the investigating authorities who were being pressed to make a judgment on the matter presented to them.)

Jan. 31, 1968 By a Decree of the Sacred Congregation for the Causes of Saints, the Process of Beatification of the Servant of God, Sister Faustina H. Kowalska is formally inaugurated.

Because of the positive outcome of the Informative Process concerning the life and virtues of Sister Faustina, inquiries from many places, especially from Poland and, in particular, from the Archbishop of Krakow, Cardinal Wojtyla, are received by the Sacred Congregation for the Doctrine of Faith, asking whether the prohibitions of the 1959 "Notification" are still in effect.

Oct. 16, 1978 Karol Cardinal Wojtyla of Krakow, Poland, becomes Pope John Paul II.

March 14, 1979 In his first encyclical, *Redemptor Hominis*, John Paul II describes the divine and human dimension of the mystery of redemption as the revelation of love which is also described as mercy. "This revelation of love and mercy has taken a form and a name: that of Jesus Christ." He is the redeemer of "each and every" man — fully revealing man to himself.

June 3, 1979 John Paul II addresses the vast assembly before the Image of the Merciful Savior, Warsaw, Poland. Cardinal Macharski asks the Marian Helpers

Center in Stockbridge, Massachusetts to bring a prayer card of this event for him to distribute.

July 12, 1979 The Congregation of Marians, having asked for an authoritative explanation of the "Notification" of 1978, receives a reply from the Prefect of the Sacred Congregation, stating that:

> *...with the new "Notification," -- ...arrived at in the light of original documentation examined also by the careful informative intervention of the then Archbishop of Krakow, Karol Cardinal Wojtyla, it was the intention of the Holy See to revoke the prohibition contained in the preceding "Notification" of 1959 -- ...there no longer exists, on the part of this Sacred Congregation, any impediment to the spreading of the devotion to The Divine Mercy in the authentic forms proposed by the Religious Sister mentioned above [the Servant of God, Sister Faustina Kowalska].*

Nov. 30, 1980 Pope John Paul II publishes his second encyclical letter *Rich in Mercy, (Dives in Misericordia)* in which he *stresses that Jesus Christ has revealed God, who is rich in mercy, as Father. He speaks of mercy as "the most stupendous attribute of the Creator and Redeemer"* (#13). Describing the mercy of God as the presence of love which is greater than evil, greater than sin, and greater than death, he summons the Church to plead for God's mercy on the whole world (#15).

In this encyclical on the mercy of God, John Paul II opens with a statement and a summary of the message: *"God who is rich in mercy, Jesus Christ reveals as Father."* He appeals to the Church to plead for God's mercy as the only answer to our present human condition. He devotes one section of the encyclical to Mary, as Mother of Mercy.

May 13, 1981 Pope John Paul II, wounded by an attempted assassination, forgives his assassin on the way to the hospital. The Diary of Sister Faustina is read to him in Polish during his convalescence.

Nov. 22, 1981 Pope John Paul II makes his first public visit outside of Rome following his lengthy recuperation, on the Feast of Christ the King, to the Shrine of Merciful Love in Collevalenza near Todi, Italy, where, within a few days, an international congress is to be held to reflect on the Encyclical *Dives in Misericordia (Rich in Mercy)* one year after its publication.

After celebrating the Holy Sacrifice of the Eucharist, he makes a strong public declaration about the importance of the message of mercy:

A year ago I published the encyclical **Dives in Misericordia.** *This circumstance made me come to the Sanctuary of Merciful Love today. By my presence I wish to reconfirm, in a way, the message of that encyclical. I wish to read it again and deliver it again.*

Right from the beginning of my ministry in St. Peter's See in Rome, I considered this message my special task. Providence has assigned it to me in the present situation of man, the Church and the world. It could be said that precisely this situation assigned that message to me as my task before God.

Feb. 25, 1983 The Holy See is approached with the petition to authorize, during the Holy Year of Redemption, the celebration of a Votive Mass of The Divine Mercy in the Diocese of Rome with the formulary already approved for the Archdiocese of Krakow. The request is granted.

Dec. 27, 1983 Pope John Paul II visits Ali Agca in his prison to extend his forgiveness. A world-wide witness to mercy, recorded in the film *Time for Mercy.*

Feb. 11, 1984 In the apostolic exhortation *Salvifici Dolores,* John Paul II describes Jesus transforming suffering by His love and mercy into the work of our salvation, and how Jesus invites us to join with Him in our suffering by our love and mercy, bringing salvation to souls. We learn from Jesus a two-fold approach of mercy to suffering: to do good *with* our suffering, and to do good *to* the suffering.

May 18, 1986 In the third encyclical of a trilogy on the Holy Trinity, *Dominum et Vivificantem,* John Paul II describes how the Holy Spirit continues the work of Jesus and he pictures Him as mercy "personified and actualized in a transcendent way..." (#39). The Holy Spirit also convinces the world of sin, not to condemn it, but to bring it to the source of all love, mercy, and salvation: the Cross, in order that we may have life. John Paul II exhorts us to implore the Holy Spirit to renew the face of the earth.

Nov. 13, 1986 Pope John Paul II is presented an icon of The Divine Mercy from the Congregation of Marians of the Immaculate Conception "as an expression of our thanksgiving for your proclaiming to the world the message of Divine Mercy." (Filmed for the movie, *Divine Mercy — No Escape,* in the apartment of the Holy Father.)

March 25, 1987 In his encyclical, *Redemptoris Mater,* on the Blessed Virgin Mary in the life of the pilgrim Church, John Paul II describes Mary as the faithful virgin and mother at Christ's first coming and as "Mediatrix of Mercy" at His final coming.

Dec. 7, 1990 In the encyclical, *Redemptoris Missio*, John

Paul II describes the mission of Christ as making the kingdom of God present, which is to make God's mercy present and believable. It is the Holy Spirit that makes mercy present. The mission of Christ is the mission of the Church.

Feb. 12, 1991 All the documents concerning the heroic virtue of Sister Faustina are completed and sent to the Sacred Congregation.

April 10, 1991 Pope John Paul II, at his general audience, speaks about Sister Faustina, showing his great respect for her, relating her to his encyclical, Rich in Mercy, and emphasizing her role in bringing the message of mercy to the world:

> *The words of the encyclical on Divine Mercy (Dives in Misericordia) are particularly close to us. They recall the figure of the Servant of God, Sister Faustina Kowalska. This simple woman religious particularly brought the Easter message of the merciful Christ closer to Poland and the whole world... .*

> *And today? ... Is it perhaps not necessary to translate into the language of today's generations the words of the Gospel, "Blessed are the merciful, for they shall obtain mercy"? (Mt 5:7)*

March 7, 1992 In the presence of the Holy Father, the Congregation for the Causes of Saints promulgates the Decree of Heroic Virtues, by which the Church acknowledges that Sister Faustina practiced all the Christian virtues to an heroic degree. As a result, she receives the title "Venerable" Servant of God, and the way is opened for verification of the miracle attributed to her intercession.

Oct. 11, 1992 In *Fidei Depositum*, John Paul II introduces the *Catechism of the Catholic Church* which is a compendium and "symphony" of our faith. It begins with God's mercy and continues throughout describing God's mercy and our response of trust in Him.

Dec. 21, 1992 The Holy Father publishes the Church's acceptance of the miracle as granted through the intercession of Sister Faustina and announces the date for her solemn beatification.

April 18, 1993 Sister Faustina is beatified by Pope John Paul II in Rome on the Second Sunday of Easter (which Our Lord had revealed to her as the "Feast of Mercy"):

*I clearly feel that my mission does not end with death, but begins," Sister Faustina wrote in her diary. And it truly did! Her mission continues and is yielding astonishing fruit. It is truly marvelous how her devotion to the merciful Jesus is spreading in our contemporary world and gaining so many human hearts! This is doubtlessly a **sign of the times — a sign of our 20th century.** The balance of this century which is now ending, in addition to the advances which have often surpassed those of preceding eras, presents a deep restlessness and fear of the future. Where, if not in The Divine Mercy, can the world find refuge and the light of hope? Believers understand that perfectly.*

Give thanks to the Lord, for He is good.

Give thanks to the Lord, for He is merciful.

Aug. 6, 1993 In his encyclical, *Veritatis Splendor,* John Paul II deals with certain fundamental questions of the Church's moral teaching. He concludes the encyclical by entrusting all the questions and the research of moralists to Mary, Mother of God and Mother of Mercy. He then explains how she is Mother of Mercy.

Aug. 14, 1993 The helicopter carrying John Paul II hovers over the 100-ft. high Image of The Divine Mercy upon departing the *World Youth Day*, Denver, Colorado.

Sept. 4, 1993 Pope John Paul II prays the Rosary at the Shrine of Ostra Brama in Vilnius, Lithuania, before the icon of the Mother of Mercy.

Sept. 5, 1993 John Paul II kneels and prays at the Image of Divine Mercy (painted under the direction of Sister Faustina) in the Church of the Holy Spirit in Vilnius, Lithuania.

April 10, 1994 Second Sunday of Easter, *Regina Caeli* Address:

What is mercy if not the boundless love of God, who confronted with human sin, restrains the sentiment of severe justice and, allowing Himself to be moved by the wretchedness of His creatures, spurs Himself to the total gift of self, in the Son's cross? 'O happy fault... which gained for us so great a Redeemer!' (Easter Proclamation).

Who can say he is free from sin and does not need God's mercy? As people of this restless time of ours, wavering between the emptiness of self-exaltation and the humiliation of despair, we have a greater need than ever for a regenerating experience of mercy.

April 1994 In *Crossing the Threshold of Hope*, Pope John Paul II answers questions submitted to him using the theme "Do not be afraid" — because the Son of God has become a man. How do we cross the threshold of hope? By trust in Jesus. He is mercy — "Love that became man, Love crucified and risen, Love unceasingly present among men. It is Eucharistic Love."

Nov. 10, 1994 In the apostolic letter, *Tertio Millenio Adveniente*, John Paul II sets out an action plan to prepare for the third millennium. He challenges us to intense prayer to the Holy Spirit for the mercy to forgive, especially overcoming the obstacles to unity, in order that our witness to evangelization be real and believable.

Jan. 23, 1995 Pope John Paul II grants to the Polish bishops that the Sunday after Easter be called the Sunday of Divine Mercy — because of the need and desire of the faithful.

March 25, 1995 In the encyclical, *Evangelium Vitae,* John Paul II calls us to mobilize our consciences and unite to build a new *culture of life* in our dramatic struggle with the culture of death. The culture of life is one of mercy — a mercy which is both love-giving life and life-giving love.

April 23, 1995 Pope John Paul II celebrates Divine Mercy Sunday in Holy Spirit Church, the Shrine of Divine Mercy in Rome. (*L'Osservatore Romano*, English Edition, April 26, 1995). In his homily, he challenges us to "trust in the Lord and be Apostles of Divine Mercy."

In his *Regina Caeli* address, he speaks of the whole Octave of Easter as a single day, and the Octave Sunday as the day of thanksgiving for God's mercy, called the Sunday of Divine Mercy. He challenges us to personally *experience* this mercy in order to be merciful and forgive — and so break the spiral of violence by the miracle of forgiveness.

May 17, 1995 On the eve of his 75th birthday, John Paul II reflects with the Wednesday general audience on the central role of Divine Mercy in his life:

I am encompassing years of service on the Vatican post. I do it being aware of my human weaknesses, yet, at the same time [being] full of great faith in the magnitude of

The Divine Mercy. First of all, I renew before Christ the offer of my readiness to serve the Church as long as He wants, surrendering myself completely to His holy will. I leave to Christ the decision of how and when He wants to relieve me of this service.

May 25, 1995 In his encyclical *Ut Unum Sint,* Pope John Paul II, in the section on the *Ministry of Unity of the Bishop of Rome,* describes his ministry as a service of unity rooted in the action of Divine Mercy (#94) and heir to the ministry of Peter:

As the heir to the mission of Peter in the Church, which has been made fruitful by the blood of the Princes of the Apostles, the Bishop of Rome exercises a ministry originating in the **manifold mercy of God.** *This mercy converts hearts and pours forth the power of grace where the disciple experiences the bitter taste of his personal weakness and helplessness. The authority proper to this ministry is completely at the service of* **God's merciful plan,** *and it must always be seen in this perspective. Its power is explained from this perspective (#92).*

Associating himself with Peter's threefold profession of love, which corresponds to the earlier threefold denial, his successor knows that **he must be a sign of mercy. His is a ministry of mercy, born of an act of Christ's own mercy.** *This whole lesson of the Gospel must be constantly read anew so that the exercise of the Petrine ministry may lose nothing of its authenticity and transparency.*

The Church of God is called by Christ to manifest to a world ensnared by its sins and evil designs that, despite everything, **God in His mercy** *can convert hearts to unity and enable them to enter into communion with Him (#93).*

November 1, 1996   In *Gift and Mystery*, John Paul II calls his memoirs of 50 years of priesthood: "Singing the mercies of the Lord."

June 7, 1997   Pope John Paul II makes a pilgrimage to the Shrine of Divine Mercy in Lagiewniki, Poland (outside of Krakow) and witnesses to his personal involvement in the Divine Mercy message and devotion.

November 29, 1998 John Paul II in *Incarnationis Mysterium,* announces the Jubilee Year of 2000, calling it a "year of mercy."

April 11, 1999   John Paul II calls the Octave day of Easter, Divine Mercy Sunday.

December 20, 1999   Pope John Paul II accepts the healing of the heart of Fr. Ronald Pytel of Baltimore, MD as the miracle needed for the canonization of Sister Faustina.

March 12, 2000   John Paul II, as a Jubilee Year act of mercy, celebrates the *Universal Prayer of Confession of Sins and asking for Forgiveness.*

April 30, 2000   Pope John Paul II canonizes Saint Maria Faustina Kowalska and proclaims Divine Mercy Sunday for the universal Church.

January 6, 2001   John Paul II publishes his Apostolic Letter, *Novo Millennium Inuente*, At the Beginning of the New Millenium.

April 22, 2001   Pope John Paul II celebrates the universal feast of Divine Mercy Sunday and the first anniversary of the canonization of St. Faustina in St. Peter's Square.